Moving His Dwelling Place

Encouragement for the journey of faith

With best wishes,
John Marshall

John Marshall

O&U
Onwards & Upwards

Onwards and Upwards Publishers

4 The Old Smithy
London Road
Rockbeare,
EX5 2EA
United Kingdom.
www.onwardsandupwards.org

First edition, published in the United Kingdom by Onwards and Upwards Publishers (2021).

ISBN: 978-1-78815-921-0
Typeface: Sabon LT

About the Author

 Originally from Yorkshire, John Marshall grew up in Torquay, Devon, on the top of a hill, overlooking the town and the distant bay. He remembers the openness, the cries of gulls, a garden bursting with flowers and insects, and he was from very young in awe of the natural world and its Creator.

Having studied French and Spanish at university, he spent most of his working life in teaching. Now retired, he admits to being "spectacularly good at doing not very much". His wife agrees and once claimed that he was the only person she knew who could happily spend an entire afternoon contemplating nothing more than a blade of grass. That said, he also writes, surveys and photographs local butterflies, walks, runs and cycles, and, occasionally, does a little exploring in France and Spain, particularly in the mountains and other wild places. In the church, he especially likes praying with others, "above all on those occasions when the Lord very obviously shows up and does something wonderful".

John is married to Carol. They live in the South West, not very far from their three children and six grandchildren.

To contact the author, please write to:

John Marshall
c/o Onwards and Upwards Publishers Ltd.
4 The Old Smithy
London Road
Rockbeare
EX5 2EA

More information about the author can be found
on the book's web page:

www.onwardsandupwards.org/moving-his-dwelling-place

God is not who you think he is,

and you are not who you think you are.

Contents

Foreword by David Edwards

IT IS A GREAT PLEASURE TO COMMEND TO YOU THIS beautiful selection of reflections, poems and prayers by my dear friend John Marshall. I remember, many years ago, when I first read one of John's poems, sensing, as I still very much sense today, that John's was a gift of writing that had been given by God for a wider audience.

Since that time I have not only enjoyed reading and felt my heart lifted by many of John's pieces but have also had the pleasure of taking part in several special events at which John has read some of his wonderful poems. They have brought pleasure and encouragement to everyone present.

It is one of the dangers of our age simply to motor through life without stopping to reflect. We need help to pause and process both the delights and the trials that we experience. I know that I am not alone in thinking that John has a particular gift to come alongside others to help in this important process. John has many times helped me to regain perspective, appreciate my blessings and experience the grace of God afresh, both through time spent together as friends and through his writing. I am so pleased that many more can now be helped in this way.

I believe that as you spend unhurried time in the pages that follow you will be able to ponder God's goodness to you, cry when you need to, laugh when you need to, and receive a fresh and beautiful vision of God's amazing gift of His Son, Jesus Christ, who has been given so freely to you.

May the Lord bring His healing and encouragement to your soul as you enjoy this delightful book.

David Edwards
Cullompton, Devon
June 2021

Introduction

IT WAS THE SUMMER OF 2009, AND AT THE VERY BEGIN-
ning of our camping holiday in Brittany we found ourselves in Saint-
Pol-de-Léon, not far from Roscoff, taking a little wander around the
town and ending up, as we often do, in the church or, in this case, the
cathedral. I confess here that I'm not much of one for historic detail,
and I have been known to drift away from guided tours because their
very learned guides have wanted to tell me far too much. I prefer,
instead, the atmosphere, the grandeur, the space, the height, the *feeling*
of it, which means that I usually spend a good part of any visit gazing
at the ceiling, as if I have some physical malady that keeps my head
locked in this generally unhelpful position. But in Saint-Pol there was
something else that caught my attention: a stained-glass window
depicting, beneath the Lord in glory and seven golden candlesticks, the
person of Saint John, writer of the book of Revelation, and underneath
his image the words *Scribe ergo quae vidisti* – "So write down the things
you have seen." [Rev.1:19]

I suppose thousands of people have walked past that window and
not thought anything about it, but to me it had special meaning,
because it was at that time that two things were happening: I was
starting to be involved in prayer ministry, and I was taking my first
hesitant steps towards 'keeping a spiritual journal'. And by those
somewhat high-sounding words I mean nothing more than jotting
down noteworthy aspects of my life with the Lord: prayers and
answered prayers, insights, a word or phrase that spoke, a Bible verse
that jumped out, the first words of a possible poem, a glimpse of
something important, or a picture or a word from the Lord. Having
made the decision to write, I soon found that making a quick, simple
note of these things was essential, because if I didn't they almost always
vanished as rapidly as they had arrived. With them written down, I
could more easily reflect on them and pray into them. Patterns began
to emerge, and signs started to become clearer, and for me this
journaling has become an invaluable aid towards hearing the voice of
God rather than just his very, very faint whisper. It has been an
important part of my growing in him.

All that follows began as nothing more than a few pencilled scribbles. These poems and reflections are, if you like, a bit of the Lord's conversation with me over the past few years that I have, with time, fleshed out and made more readable. Never, though, were they intended for publication; the most I have ever done is share a few in small groups. But friends tried, and kept on trying, to encourage me to make something more of them, and I declined and kept on declining. Eventually, I came close to giving in, and I asked the Lord what he thought. A day or so later, among the prophetic words and pictures given out at our church, there was the following: a picture of a pen, and with it words that went something like, "Write down the things that you see." So I took another step, to see whether doors would open or close, and the result is what you have here. I should say, if it's not already clear, that each piece was written as a one-off item, so please don't expect them to knit together seamlessly. And do, please, read the Bible passage that I have given at the start of each piece. If the Lord is going to speak to you – and he will, if you let him – he is much more likely to do it through his own words than through mine. As for the prayers, I had not intended to write any, but I was asked by the publisher to include some, and so I have. I hope they help, but I would be glad if you were to use them only as a springboard to your own prayers, which I am sure will be fuller, more personal and much more imaginative than my own.

As I have said above, this book exists because of the encouragement and persistence of friends and family. And so my thanks to them, but to two people in particular: my friend David Edwards, for encouraging me throughout, for making several helpful suggestions regarding the text, and for lifting me up on the numerous occasions when that has been necessary, and my wife, Carol, for her gentle and constant support, and for her belief in the book and in me.

Where I have referred to other people and their stories, I have received their permission to do so. Where this hasn't been possible, I have changed names and certain details in an attempt to preserve anonymity. Where I have failed in that, I apologise, and hope that you will forgive me.

1

A Hole in the Ceiling

Mark 2:1-12

IT WAS DURING THE FIRST HYMN THAT I FELT AN EVER SO slight nudge inside me: "Ask Tony what the Lord has said to him today." I dismissed it, erring as I tend to do on the side of extreme caution. Even when a word that I have shared has resonated deeply with the other person, that word has never arrived in my ears to the accompaniment of trumpets. On this occasion there wasn't even the faint ping of a triangle, and I told myself that it wasn't going to happen. Besides, I didn't know Tony very well – not at all, actually – and I didn't want to risk embarrassing him. I didn't want to embarrass myself either.

Five minutes later we were sharing the Peace, some of us leaving our seats and wandering about a bit. I don't know what it was about Tony, maybe the very happy expression on his face, but after we'd blessed each other with the Peace, I showed an extreme lack of self-control and I blurted it out, "What has the Lord said to you today, Tony?"

"He's shown me," answered Tony, without the slightest hesitation, "that I need to be more cheerful with people; that I need to pass on an infectious smile, because so many people are going around looking at their feet." And then he smiled at me, and I couldn't help smiling too, and I'm smiling now as I write this, because the whole thing was just so funny.

It reminded me of an evening on prayer I attended six months ago which culminated in our being given a Bible passage to read. It was Mark 2:1-12, and we had specific instructions: "Read it, and then ask the Lord to reveal something to you about it." We were told not to have preconceived ideas about what we might expect; the Lord would decide what he wanted to bring to our attention. We were told not to interpret, not to theorise, and certainly not to produce a sermon on it. Our job was to sit quietly and otherwise do nothing, and we were given ten minutes in which to do it. So I read the passage, and I sat quietly, and when nothing happened I was disappointed. But then, about nine and three quarter minutes into my allotted ten, something did happen: I was overwhelmed by a sense of how wonderfully funny Jesus found it. I mean, hilarious.

The thing is, you don't get that from reading the passage, because the story appears to have a very serious tone to it. So much so that more than once, and from very reasonable and good-natured people, I have heard comments such as, "So who paid for the repairs?" as if that were the main thing here, though such comments do show us how very easy it is to align ourselves, albeit unconsciously, with the teachers of the Law in their fault-finding. In the past I may have been guilty of that too as I thought about the poor roof, but the Lord wasn't letting me find fault now. Why not? Because Jesus found it so funny, because the roof didn't matter, and because something much more important was going on.

Jesus, don't forget, had gone back home to Capernaum, so whose house was it? Was it a friend's? Was it his own? Either way, he might have had more cause to worry about the repairs than if it had been a stranger's house, but he doesn't appear to be at all worried. He doesn't throw into the drama what we ourselves might have thrown in: complaints, accusation and a great deal of anxiety. Instead, thanks to what I believe the Lord showed me, I now see Jesus roaring with laughter. The ceiling's being torn open, a man is being let down on a stretcher, and it's as if I can hear Jesus exclaiming, "Wow, I didn't know I was *that* popular!" And now the laughter is running through the crowd. It's infecting those who are wedged in the doorway. It's rippling among those outside, and it has painted huge smiles on the four faces still looking down through that hole in the roof. And what is its cause? Jesus' unashamed and uncontainable delight in seeing these men in their headlong rush towards life. They are men who mean business, who won't accept no for an answer, and who are taking a big risk in order to see their friend healed. With the doorway jammed with people, there's no point in queueing, so they show some initiative and begin to take the house apart. And Jesus loves it, and he loves them for being compassionate enough and fired up enough to do it. Predictably, though, not everybody sees the funny side.

There are all sorts of contrasts apparent in this scene. There are those who have hearts longing to see Jesus and who are stuck outside, and those whose hearts are a million miles from Jesus but who have given themselves a place of pre-eminence in the front row, the teachers

14

of the Law. Jesus exudes humour and warmth; they sit there like blocks of ice. Jesus stretches up his arms to welcome the paralysed man; the teachers sit motionless, stiff and starchy. Luckily for them, ice and starch have a certain luminosity, so at least they are going to be noticed, but then a hole appears in the roof and their light turns into darkness when compared with the poor invalid, now brightly illuminated by a shaft of sunlight which simply shouldn't be there.

For a moment the teachers of the Law may think that they should pack up and go home, but then Jesus makes his fatal mistake: he forgives the man his sins. Now the pendulum seems to have swung back again, and we see smiles appear for the first time on the teachers' faces. They have been right all along, and Jesus is wrong, and thank goodness that even in this dusty farce they can still be God for people who would otherwise not know how to know him. And so, not for the first or the last time, they sit in judgement. We thought that the only ones looking down were the four guys on the roof, but these teachers of the Law are professionals; looking down has been their life's work.

Then Jesus heals the man, and as the man leaps to his feet, I imagine the laughter being even louder than it was the first time. Laughter, joy, amazement, life in abundance and lots of smiles, not only on the faces of most of those present but on Jesus' face too, even though, as he watches the teachers of the Law skulk away, he knows that by showing everybody what God is really like, he is sowing the seeds of his own death. But still that doesn't prevent him from laughing now, along with those who, even if only in a very small way, have begun to see God more clearly than they did before.

As a youth I was familiar with Herbert Beecroft's painting 'And the Lord turned and looked upon Peter'. In the painting, Beecroft attempts to capture Jesus' expression on being denied three times by Peter. I doubt if it's a good approximation of the real thing, but more importantly, I don't think it's a helpful image of Jesus to carry in one's head as I may have done for too long. And that's because this stern Jesus made me feel bad about myself, and this wasn't necessary, because I didn't need any help in doing that. Jesus keeps his stern face for the teachers of the Law and their kind, the ones who look down on people, the ones who think they're perfect. To those of us who know we aren't, he comes with big smiles and a hug. And with uproarious laughter, as if a hole has just appeared in a dark sky and brilliant light is now pouring in, which of course it is.

EDEN

We sat in high Sahara dunes
For lunch, just Jesus and me;
And nowhere anything but pyramids of sand
And Jesus and me.
It seemed enough.
And then he held out water,
Not to me, but as an offering,
And poured the first part out upon the ground.
Strange, this water should have soaked away,
Vanished at once in that heat,
But it remained instead a little pool,
Still for a moment, then stirring,
Bubbling, springing up
To race headlong and down the dune,
Widening and deepening as it went.
Jesus smiled, as if himself surprised,
And then pulled out an offering of fruit,
Of pomegranates, dates, and figs,
And some of these he threw like cricket balls
And watched them splash
With plumes of damp sand
Down where the running stream had forked.
With barely a pause
A tree appeared, then more, which grew,
Blossomed, fruited, attracted sparrows,
Doves and sunbirds,
And all as I watched, enveloped
By this Eden recreated.
I smiled, and Jesus smiled.
"You're welcome," he said.
And that smile
And those words,
They would have been enough.

A Prayer

Jesus,
You broke through
The roof of this world
To rescue me,
To heal me, to lift me up,
And smile on me.

Jesus,
Help me never to resist
That smile you have.
Help me to smile like you;
Help me to want
To break through roofs like you do,
That others may see you smile on them
In just the same way
That you smile on me.

2

Even the Stones

Revelation 5

LAST GOOD FRIDAY MY WIFE, CAROL, AND I DECIDED TO do something different, and we went to a church closer to home. As we entered, I began to wish we hadn't, my heart sinking as each of us was given one of those pebbles that seem to be all the rage these days, and I wondered what on earth I was going to be asked to do with it. I wasn't helped by a line in my leaflet which said, "You will have an opportunity to use your pebble in the course of the service." *Oh dear*, I thought. *I hope the preacher's not too bad, because I have quite a good aim.* I was already feeling sorry for myself, and I started to feel sorry for the preacher too.

Inevitably, given the way things seem to work in my life, this pebble business was for me the most significant part of our time together. I had commented during our walk to church how odd it was that we met together on Good Friday to remember the death of someone who is very much alive. We can't escape this, but I think the vicar got it right when he said that during the Easter weekend we shouldn't rush too quickly into Easter Sunday. Not because we pretend on Good Friday that Jesus is still dead, but because Good Friday gives us another opportunity to stay a while considering, among other things, the importance of Jesus' death: what it was, what it achieved, what it meant and what it still means.

And one of the things that his death still means is that having endured the pain of the cross, Jesus is able not only to identify with and share my own pain but also to carry it, and there in that Good Friday service we were encouraged to consider some painful burden that we might be carrying and then to take our little pebble, now representing this painful thing, and lay it by the large wooden cross stretched out on the stone floor of the church, asking Jesus to lift the weight of the burden from us. A little pebble for a big boulder, if you like. I, for one, had no difficulty in identifying a painful burden, and once I'd plucked up the courage necessary to get up out of my seat I had no difficulty either in setting it next to the cross. But having the faith to believe that Jesus could and would lift it was more difficult, especially when I saw the layer of stones getting bigger, pebble by pebble, each falling on another with a little click, like the ticking of a clock. *That was a lot of burdens*, I thought, and I couldn't help asking the Lord if he was sufficient, if he was really up to the task. His reply was simple: "I am."

So it was good not to rush into Easter Sunday, because there was something special in that particular place at that particular time, as I suppose there always is. "I was interested to see," the speaker began, commenting on the pile of pebbles, "that my stone was bigger this year than it was last year." Indeed. And this year the burden that we bring may be bigger than last year's. Next year's may be bigger still. It doesn't matter, because the Lord is always sufficient. You'll be tempted to believe that he isn't, but he is. At the end of the service the cross was lifted up and carried from the church. Left behind, on the stone floor, was a cross-shaped space outlined in small pebbles. It was beautiful, and very moving.

Some time after this, as I was reflecting on the cross and on my burden, I had a picture in my mind of Jesus standing at the foot of his cross; his hands were open and his arms were outstretched to a crowd of people gathered around him in a big circle but still at some distance from him. These people were all carrying large burdens, either on their backs or on their shoulders or in their arms like sacks of cement. They stood in the shadows, and Jesus, who was in bright sunlight, was inviting them to step forward so that he could take their burdens from them. But strangely, no one moved, and I remember feeling some sadness over this, not principally because there are so many people carrying burdens unnecessarily, since that might be simply out of ignorance, but because many are carrying burdens even though they know that Jesus' great desire is to take these loads from them. In part this may be because they are wondering, as I had done, whether Jesus really is up to the task, but I suspect it's also because, bizarrely, many of us become attached to the burdens we're carrying and can't imagine life, or ourselves, without them. We don't love them, but we don't want to be rid of them either, perhaps because they go some way towards providing us with an excuse for being who we are. Stepping forward into the light of the cross, especially if we're not seeing, or if we're choosing not to see, the joyful, welcoming expression on Jesus' face, can seem the most difficult thing on earth. It's much easier to stay where we are, even if that means staying in the gloom.

Not long ago we were praying with a young woman who was experiencing a lot of resentment over something that a member of her family had done. She knew that this resentment wasn't healthy, either emotionally or spiritually, but although her desire was to give it to the Lord, her will was strongly opposed to this. As often happens in such situations, she was listening to the voice that says, "Your resentment is your protection, your rightful defence, your guard against further hurt. Who knows what might happen if you let it go? And anyway, if you do let it go, the other person wins. Is that what you want?"

"Are you willing," I asked, "to see what Jesus has to say about that?" She was, and so we asked. Usually, once Jesus has brought his truth and exposed the protective lie as nothing more than hot air, we can move towards offering up the resentment. This time, however, and to my astonishment and great pleasure, the Lord simply took over. At the very moment when the young woman stepped into the light of the cross and said yes to hearing Jesus, the expression on her face changed completely, and I sat back and waited. A bit later she explained. "As soon as I'd said yes to Jesus, I had two pictures in my head. The first was of the person I resented, but as I looked at him I understood how good and supportive and loyal he's been to me. The second picture was me, and I understood that over the years I haven't treated him anything like as well. Despite that, I had no sense of condemnation from the Lord. He was simply showing me the real picture and not the false one that I'd been seeing."

"And what about your resentment?" I asked.

"Gone," she said, "as if it was never there. It was so strong before, and now I don't feel any of it."

I happened to meet the young woman a week later, and I asked her how she was. "It hasn't come back," she said. "To be honest, I've tried to make it come back, as a sort of experiment, but I can't. It's gone." Jesus, it seems, will gladly lift from us those loads we don't need to carry if only we will give them up to him. And those things we do need to carry? Well, he'll take most of their weight himself.

"Come to me, all of you who are tired from carrying heavy loads, and I will give you rest. Take my yoke and put it on you, and learn from me, because I am gentle and humble in spirit; and you will find rest. For the yoke I will give you is easy, and the load I will put on you is light." [Matt.11:28-30]

HIS DANCING EYES

It is not his condemnation
That most frightens me;
It's his open invitation.

He says, "Let go of what you're thinking.
Walk on water."
I think I'm sinking.

The scary bit – here's the surprise –
Is not a cold, forbidding face,
But laughing, dancing eyes.

"I'm here for the sick not the well,"
He says. What irony.
'Well', meaning 'well on the way to hell'.

"It isn't the respectable
I'm calling." See me stalling:
Respectable is my commendable.

From my sheltered, warm cocoon
He invites me to step out.
Easier crawling to the moon.

How strange they sit so far apart,
My will and my desire.
So many walls around my heart,

And a line drawn here at my feet.
I'm on this side; he's over there,
Standing unburned in fiery furnace heat.

A Prayer

Jesus,
I know who you are,
And that frightens me.
You say, "Come to me,"
And I shrink back.
You say, "Don't be afraid,"
And I tremble.
You say, "Trust me,"
And I hesitate.

Jesus,
You know who I am,
But that doesn't stop you loving me.
You know that stepping out is difficult,
But you reach out your hand to me.
You know I find it very hard to trust,
But I will risk my trust in you,
Because I do know who you are:
I know that you are good, and I will trust
That I am safe with you.

3

Calling Us Friends

John 15:1-17

ONE OF THE PRIVILEGES OF PRAYER MINISTRY IS THAT IT allows us to be involved, in a very minor way, in other people's stories. Their stories are, by necessity, unique. They vary one from another in their details, both great and small, but there are often important similarities in terms of theme, and the other evening at home group I decided to try a little experiment.

I explained to the group that I was going to ask them to still themselves, to close their eyes and to answer, without overthinking anything, a couple of questions. I insisted that they were not to worry about right or wrong answers, because no answer was wrong if it was honest. And I also tried to calm any fears they might have had about reporting back to the group. It was fine if they did, and it was fine if they didn't. So, when they appeared settled, I asked the first question: "When you look at yourself, what do you see?" Then, after about a minute, I asked the second: "And when Jesus looks at you, what does he see?" And then, in the stillness, and without any certainty about what was going to happen, I offered a silent prayer. And I may have crossed my fingers.

I'm hoping at this point that before I tell you what happened next, you will ask yourself the same questions and pause for a moment to let yourself answer them, because they are important questions, and you do need to know what your answers are. As for the group, their responses fell broadly into the two possibilities that from experience I had been expecting. Firstly, there were those who, when they looked at themselves, didn't see a great deal to like. They saw what they saw in the mirror – drooping eyes, greying hair, sagging flesh, spots – and then all the internal stuff that keeps these things company: unrealised hopes, broken relationships, disappointments, failure. And when they were asked what Jesus saw when he looked at them, their answer wasn't very different: he saw much the same thing.

The other type of answer was in some ways similar but it contained one all-important difference: when Jesus looked at them, he looked at them with eyes brimming over with love and without any hint of condemnation. He treasured them. He was their very best friend, and they were his. They may still have seen their own greying hair and may still have had a sense of their own failures, but these things had been transformed by what they saw when they looked at Jesus and when they saw him looking back at them, so that these negative things had therefore lost their power to influence and control.

It occurred to me then that I could very usefully devote the rest of my life to letting people know what Jesus sees when he looks at them. And I'm not talking only about people outside the church, I'm also talking about the ones inside it – the ones who should know better because they've been told a thousand times from the pulpit, but who just won't allow themselves to believe the good news; the ones who, after a lifetime in the church, still look at themselves and see nothing but a dismal, unattractive failure and assume that Jesus must see the same; the ones who believe that Jesus couldn't possibly want them as a friend; the ones who, when you ask them if they love the Lord, reply, "I do my best."

Most of us are desperate to get out of school, but we never really leave it. "Does his best", "fair effort", "could try harder". All those comments in all those reports live on in us, so that when teachers are no longer reporting on us, we continue their work by reporting on ourselves. The list gets longer and longer, and when Jesus says to us, as he says to the woman caught in adultery, "I don't condemn you either," we don't really believe him. Well, that's not quite true; maybe we believe it in our heads, because the vicar says it too, but in our hearts we know a deeper truth, and it's this truth that always wins. It's the truth that says, "I can't be a friend of Jesus, because why would Jesus want a friend like me?" We desperately want grace, but the law has a habit of winning, because we've grown so comfortable with it. We feel naked without it, and who would want to see us naked? Only the other day, when I asked a lady about her friendship with Jesus, she said, "I get so confused between the Old and the New Testaments, between law and grace." In other words, "I don't think I deserve his friendship."

No, of course she didn't. And neither do you or I, but you never deserve friendship. Friendship comes because the other person wants to give it, because they have a heart for friendship, and because they look at you and see something much bigger and much better than any surface imperfections that might be there and which you can't take your eyes off. They see something that appeals, something that attracts, something that they want to connect with, and in that connecting, in that sharing, the very best of you will blossom, and the very best of the other person will blossom too, Jesus included. Jesus wants you to be his friend because he loves you, and in this friendship that he wants to have with you, you will become more yourself and, though it's hard to believe, he will become more himself too.

Try to remember this: the full weight of the law was laid on Jesus, so that the full weight of grace could be laid on you. Yes, even you!

Ten Things I Appreciate About You

When you smile,
You lift off my gravestone mask,
And when it falls,
It breaks in pieces noisily
Around my startled feet.

When you say, "Well done,"
I stand a little taller,
And the space once occupied
By lack of confidence
Gives back a portion of the rent I pay.

When you cry with me,
I see, in exquisite miniature,
Two people squeezed together
In one single tear
Become inseparable.

When you forgive me,
You help me shed a hundred heavy coats,
And child-light I step out
And walk away, with not
One thought of looking back.

When you understand me,
I open every cupboard in the house
And discover that my dark possessions
Have all been scattered out
For sparrows and for doves.

When you sing,
A champagne glass
Begins to fill,
And bubbles rise and burst
In me like fireworks.

When you place your hand on mine,
You force me to unpick
The tapestries of insecurity and fear
That I have so painstakingly
Assembled.

When you embrace me,
You take this empty jar of mine
And you fill it up
To overflowing with the fragrant oil
Of your joy and your strength.

When you pray with me,
You catch me floating
In a room filled with space debris,
And you bring me
Gently back to earth.

When you come into the house,
You take the little light there is
And you multiply it
Till our faces shine, and when you leave,
Twelve baskets full of fire are burning still.

A PRAYER

Lord,
You do not ask that I fill my life with successes,
But that I fill my weaknesses
With your strengths, and that I fill
My failings with your forgiveness.
You do not commend me for my independence,
But for my courage in asking for help
And my willingness to accept it.
And you do not praise me
For striking out on my own,
For reaching the end of my life only to declare,
Proudly, "I did it my way!"

You commend me, instead,
For my readiness to walk with others,
And for allowing others to walk with me.
You commend me
Not for eating alone in my small corner,
But for breaking bread with those around me.
You commend me
For being prepared to make friends,
For being a friend,
For wanting friends,
Just as Jesus himself
Wanted friends,
Wants friends still,
And calls us friends.

4

Walking in the Garden

Genesis 3:1-13

THIS MORNING I WAS ONCE AGAIN THINKING OF HOW well some of my fellow university students have done in life. One is now a bishop, another is a top barrister, some work in the Home Office, and doubtless several are millionaires. Of course it's perfectly possible that others have known a lifetime of unemployment, have lived in loveless marriages or are despised by their children. At least one has passed on. Nevertheless, as always with me, I wasn't dwelling on the latter and on my comparative good fortune. I was dwelling on the big achievers and on the great things that they have done – and that I haven't done.

My heavenly Father, as always with him, saw things from a different perspective. "When you spent yesterday afternoon with your grand-daughters, which bit did you enjoy most?" This wasn't the first time I'd heard the queen hit the chessboard with a click that was gentle but firm, and I knew it was another checkmate to him. The answer to his question was that we'd gone to the park – our regular Sunday afternoon fixture that I will miss like crazy when the girls are too old to want to – and we'd played tennis, and rounders, and boules. And we'd swung on the swings, and we'd climbed on the ropes and on the logs, and we'd eaten a whole packet of cheese biscuits. But the bit I enjoyed most was none of these things. It was the moment almost at the end, after we'd delivered them safely home, when my eldest grand-daughter snuggled up to me on the settee and told me, for about fifteen seconds, what she'd most enjoyed about her recent holiday. And then she was up and off, off to do something more pressing, something more interesting.

I think that one of the reasons God gives us relationships with people is so that we can better understand our relationship with him. Relationships are like mirrors, although, as so often with mirrors, we may not like what we see. And what I see is me giving the Lord his fifteen seconds, or maybe even fifteen minutes of my time, and then dashing off to something more urgent, something that really needs to be done, when what he most wants is for me to snuggle up, let him put his arm around me, tell him about my day, what's excited me, what's disappointed me, what I'm hoping for, what I need help with. Because he longs to be involved. As my father. As my mother. He might even have something to share with me.

The invitation is always there to steal away to Jesus, to steal away home, but we set such little store by it, imagining instead that in order to please him we have to do, to work, to achieve. We are happy to trot out the old line that says the devil finds work for idle hands, not realising that he also finds work for busy hands. Snuggling up to the Lord is not the same as being idle. It can require a real act of the will. Battles often have to be fought before snuggling can happen, because the end result is so precious. It's a delight that the enemy would rather we did without. Busyness, on the other hand, can simply be another form of idleness. It's very easy to drift, unthinking, into busyness.

Blessed are those who love to snuggle up. "Come near to God, and he will come near to you," it says in James 4. In other words, "Snuggle up!" Many know from experience how the Lord pours out his Spirit in greater measure during or after very beautiful times of corporate worship. From that, our logical minds can fall into another trap, that of thinking that in order to experience his presence we have to do the worship thing first, and preferably lots of it, as if it were some sort of duty. Wouldn't it be much better to see worship as a time of snuggling? "Snuggle up to me, and I will snuggle up to you." The Lord doesn't give himself to us simply because we've done something dutifully. He gives himself to us because we've wanted to snuggle up and because we've enjoyed snuggling up. He doesn't pour out his Spirit as a reward for a good job done. His Spirit is poured out because the Lord is enjoying himself, because he's enjoying our company and expressing his joy in our relationship. In short, because he's snuggling up too.

The Lord wants me to snuggle up to him even though I'm not a bishop. In fact he's not at all bothered that I'm not a bishop, and he would, if I asked him, give me a hundred reasons why my being a bishop would have been a very bad idea. But he is bothered about my snuggling up to him, and he seems to put it right at the top of his list of priorities and pleasures, even though I have to work very hard to let that thought even begin to sink in.

One morning recently, as I was praying, an image came into my mind. I was with Jesus, and he was holding out his closed hands towards me. "Choose a hand," he said. I pointed to his right hand, which he opened. In it was an extraordinary collection of famous buildings in miniature: the Eiffel Tower, a pyramid, Buckingham Palace and many more, each tightly pressed against the next. I couldn't take my eyes off them, they were so beautiful. Then Jesus blew on them, very gently. His breath was barely strong enough to feel, but as it reached his hand, the buildings crumbled and became nothing more than dust, which then blew away, leaving his hand empty. I nodded towards his other hand, which again he opened. In that hand, again in miniature, I saw Jesus and me, sitting very close together, talking. Seeing ourselves so small was even stranger than seeing the tiny buildings. And now he did the same thing again; he blew gently on his hand. I half expected to share the fate of the buildings, but no. This time, as he breathed out, the two of us began to glow like hot coals, and with each breath we burned brighter and brighter. And then he stopped, and the redness started to disappear. Of course, coals turn grey and become ash, but we didn't. After the cooling we remained exactly as we had started, just the two of us talking together.

On that fateful day in Eden, Adam and Eve heard the Lord walking in the garden, and they hid from him. And then those three poignant words... "Where are you?" We concentrate, of course, on the fall from grace, on death and pain, on all that Adam and Eve lost. But what about what God lost? Hadn't they been walking together each evening, talking, reminiscing perhaps, planning the day ahead and enjoying each other's company? Hadn't they been snuggling up? "Where are you?" really means, "Where are my friends that I've lost, because I really miss them?"

STANDING ROOM ONLY

I like to pray alone,
But now and then I fear
That I'm the only one at home.
I like to pray aloud,
But sometimes comes the doubt
That nobody's about
To hear my prayers, my groans, my shouts.
It's not a dialogue at all;
I'm bouncing words off these four walls,
Their echoes coming back as taunts,
So even when I'm kneeling,
I have that disconcerting feeling
I may be speaking to the ceiling,
Not smiling, but frowning,
Not praying, but drowning,
And no-one comes to sit with me
On my comfy, two-seater,
Shabby-chic settee.

But what if, when I pray,
My Father is already there,
And I'm the one who's unaware?
What if he arrived while still I slept,
Tiptoed in, prepared the room, all well before
I shambled from the bedroom door?
What if, when I sit to pray, settle,
Fidget and shuffle at the starting line,
Watch the minutes ticking past, and
Take a sip of tea as if it were my last,
What if my Father has run to meet me there,
Has been running since before dawn,
Since before I was born,
And still has time to make his everything
This little box I set aside,
Perhaps begrudgingly, for prayer?
What if he has been
On the edge of his seat,

Waiting anxiously to see
If I'll show up, not daring to believe
That I might want to share my heart with him
As he would like to share his heart with me?
And what if my Lord's excitement
Runs through his angels like a song?
What if they crowd my living room
To listen in, to catch a glimpse
Of this extraordinary thing?
What if they snuggle by the fireplace,
Perch, legs dangling, on the mantelpiece,
Sit cross-legged on every inch of floor,
Squeeze one behind another by the door?
What if my sense of being lonely,
This tempting, empty-room confusion,
Turns out to be the real illusion?
What if this vacant space I think I see
Is full to bursting, so that
Even for angels,
There is standing room only?

A PRAYER

Lord, forgive me
When you have called me over in love,
And I have excused myself with busyness.
Lord, forgive me
When you have tried to grow your gifts in me,
And I have run after medals and monuments.
Lord, forgive me
When I have dwelt too long on things not done
And believe that I am worth much less to you.
Lord, forgive me
When I have scorned the opportunity for treasures in heaven
And sought instead to pile them up on earth.

Call to me again, Lord.
Breathe peace into my busyness,
And calm my hunger for achievement.
Give me the desire to pause,
To take time, to stop,
To desire nothing but this present, quiet
Stillness with my God.

5

The Strange Beauty of Giraffes

Genesis 1:24-31; Proverbs 3:5-6

OUR SON WORKS IN GRAPHIC DESIGN; THE CREATIVE, artistic impulse runs strong in him, as it does in each of our three children. Away from work, and as means of relaxing, he combs local beaches in search of shards of pottery, and with the pieces that he finds he creates works of art. He's good at it, and I think his creations are beautiful to look at. Trouble is, he works on a rather large scale, which means that each piece takes a lot of time to produce. Earlier this year he casually dropped into conversation that he was thinking how useful it would be if he could find someone with the time to give him a little help. He would complete the basic design, and his helper would fill in all the less interesting bits. So I volunteered.

I have now helped him with five pieces, and I have found it great fun to do. Others I have spoken to have said how they wouldn't have the time or the skill or, much more importantly, the patience. And I understand that; sometimes I have taken an hour to glue on only half a dozen pieces. But I have loved it. I place the unfinished picture on the table, surround it with hundreds of unused shards, each one brimming with possible usefulness, put on some music, and away I go, off into a world of my own, a world that is both empty and full – empty, because I don't have to think about anything; and full, because the creative spirit takes over and begins to work its magic.

And sometimes it really does appear to be magic, because I always have the strangest feeling that despite it being my hands that pick up and stick on each piece, the work is somehow in the process of creating itself. For starters, it soon became clear to me that for the most part there isn't 'one right piece'. Very often it's a matter of trawling through and trying dozens of possibly suitable shards and then trusting the best fit. An even better fit might exist in the still sizeable bag of bits on the floor, but if I looked in there too, nothing would ever get done; the search for the perfect piece could go on for ever. I place my trust in what is there to be worked with. Having said that, sometimes a near perfect piece simply appears in front of my eyes, with no searching at all, and this is always a pleasure. At other times the piece that I think I am looking for, and which I eventually find, turns out not to be the piece that I really need; the piece I need looks nothing like the one I thought I wanted. Often a square piece looks best in a round hole, the hole and the piece having seemed completely incompatible before I put them together.

It's not all plain sailing. Occasionally the matching up of a piece with a gap can become very frustrating, and then I say, "Lord, find the piece for me before I go mad!" Often I then find it very quickly, but this doesn't always happen, and I am forced to carry on looking. If this really is God's doing, I have no idea why he sometimes answers like this and why he sometimes doesn't. More importantly, no matter how perfect and how God-given the piece may be, it's still a piece that creates another gap, a gap which will need filling by one more piece that as yet I haven't even begun to guess at. And I have come to see it as the story of my life.

We were talking about this very thing at home group yesterday evening, about how our affirming that the Lord has directed our paths can be harder for those with a somewhat chequered career history (or, indeed, life history) than for those who very early on were aware of their calling and were able to follow it through unhindered. And I am again helped by sea pottery. It's as I said earlier: apart from a very basic idea and the bare bones of the design, by and large the work creates itself. Of course, it's my fingers at work, and after much trial and error it's my own choice of piece to insert, but even five minutes earlier I had not the least idea which piece I would be needing and certainly not a clue as to the size of the gap that would need to be filled after that. The finished work can therefore never be what I had intended it to be, because *in its detail* it was impossible for me to intend anything. So the result is always a surprise, always a delight and always – and I do mean *always* – better than I had previously imagined.

What if God, in the creation of the world, does the same thing? What if, when a giraffe finally came together, the Lord exclaimed, "Wow, I didn't expect it to be as weirdly beautiful as that!" What if, when he looks at you, he says, "Wow, you've turned out to be even lovelier than I had imagined!" And that, of course is warts and all, because I have learned the hard way that superglue has the final say, in that when I have occasionally tried to remove a poorly chosen piece, I have usually damaged other pieces in the process. From now on, once it's stuck, it's stuck. It follows, then, that the final picture includes those pieces that haven't fitted perfectly, and that's most of them, the square bits that probably should have been round, the sharp bits that would have been better smooth, the big bits that could have been smaller, and the small bits that could have been bigger. It includes the stumbles, the indecisions and the poor decisions, the several changes of direction, and the mistakes big and small. It includes the lot.

But here's the thing: when the picture is at last complete – and it can take a long time – I find myself poring over it, marvelling at so many surprises, nearly all of which are to do with seeing for the first time how effective, and how lovely, one small, previously insignificant, even possibly wrong piece appears now that it glories in the context of the whole. This one tiny piece completes the beauty of the entire image, and the entire image completes the beauty of this one tiny piece. Best of all is when the picture is framed and hung on the wall. It's then that I can stand back and say to myself, "Wow, not long ago that picture was nothing more than bits of rubbish on a beach. Just look at it now!"

What if God is saying something similar about my chequered life? Or about yours? What if, in your regrets over a lack of perceived calling or over a catalogue of poor life choices, you are failing to appreciate the beauty that a life given to God – even after or in the middle of the poor life choices – will have when he glues all the pieces together? Because right now you simply don't know just how much light shone off the word of encouragement you gave to that child struggling at school. You can't begin to guess at the way in which the Lord's gaze rested on the casual visit you made to the person who in that moment needed to feel that they mattered, and you have already forgotten that morning when you resisted an attitude of harshness and chose instead to be gracious and forgiving. For you and me these things can be all too easily passed off, or passed by like bits of broken pottery on a pebbly beach. But let's remember that the Lord delights in them, and he collects up every single one, not simply because for him each one has the potential for great beauty but also because he has a very good idea, in a way that we simply cannot have, of what the finished picture will one day look like.

I was talking to the Lord recently about prayer ministry, and I was asking him, in a probably complaining and immature sort of way, why there was so much variety in the results. In other words, why did people sometimes show an obvious, even dramatic response to being prayed for, while on other occasions nothing much or absolutely nothing at all appeared to happen? If I expected an answer to this, which I may not have done, it would have gone something like, "You need to get up at five in the morning and pray harder, John." But I did get an answer, and it was so very different from that stern reply, being much more gentle and generous, and, of course, much more him. It was said, as it sometimes is when I'm being immature and complaining, with a slightly raised eyebrow, "It's not a factory, John. I'm not producing cans of beans, I'm creating works of art."

THE YOU THAT YOU ARE

I'm asking you to be you
And not try to be me.
Will you let me be me,
As I let you be you?
I made you to be you,
And I'm happy with you –
The you that you are,
That you were and will be –
So please shake off the pressure
Of trying to be me.
And as for those others
You think better than you –
The ones you believe
Have a much closer view –
I'll say it again
And again and again:
I called you by name,
And I love you the same.
So take it easy, relax,
Accept your own skin;
I made it on purpose
For just you to live in.
Be kind to yourself,
Accept that it's true
That my heart is to shine
A bit differently through you –
A less fiery red, but a deeper sea blue
Which no-one, that's no-one,
I'd let share with you.
Do away with comparisons,
Don't put yourself down;
Try inwardly happy,
Don't inwardly frown.
I will work through your strengths
And your weaknesses too;
And those flaws which are yours –
So peculiar to you –

I'll transform, if you let me,
And turn them to good,
Just as someone who loves you
Abundantly would.
So don't wrap yourself up
And sit tight on the shelf;
Don't look down at your shoes
And belittle yourself.
Remember I made you;
Your gifts were my choice:
Your hands and your thinking,
Your dreaming, your voice.
And while hard to take in,
Please remember it's true:
I can't do all that I do
If I haven't got you.

A PRAYER

Is this what I think, Lord,
That it's too good to be true?
I, who each morning
Dress myself in the old lies
For the new day,
Listening at every moment
To all the wrong voices,
And placing huge bets
On my own failures.
Is this what I think,
That these lies are the truth,
And the truth nothing more
Than a handful
Of faded clichés?

The truth
Is the war that I'm in,
And the battles being fought over me.
The truth
Is the price that was paid,
Declaring me loved
And setting me free.
The truth
Is a heart that is good
And a light
That shines out of me.
The truth
Is the song
That is sung over me,
Beautifully,
Ceaselessly,
Calling my name.

6

As Good As It Gets

Psalm 63

IT'S AUGUST, AND I AM SITTING ON A BEACH IN NORTHERN Brittany. For years some friends of ours spent their summer holidays here. They caught the ferry to Roscoff and then drove for about half an hour. That close. Carol and I could never understand it. Why not go further south, explore a bit, get some sun, do something different? Their lack of adventurous spirit never ceased to amaze us. We didn't understand them at all, but now we do.

Our beach is set in a little bay, linked by low, rocky headlands to other little bays and coves which stretch along the entire coast. At low tide the rocks and tiny islands are spectacular. I can truly say that I have never seen as many rocks as I can see at this moment; they stretch out on both sides and sit in the bay ahead of me, breaking up the sea into random but beautiful patterns. Surprisingly, since we are only about a hundred miles from Plymouth, the sea is the colour of the Mediterranean, a deep, rich blue where there are submarine rocks and a bright turquoise over the pale sand. These bands of different blue run out to the horizon where yachts tilt against the wind. To my right, strings of rocks looking like the backs of partially submerged dinosaurs make a natural harbour, and a score of small boats of all colours bob at their moorings. The sky is only a little paler than the sea, and far away I can pick out a low bank of cloud showing me where England is.

Under my feet the sand is fine and a light silver beige. Specks of it glint in the bright sun, and if you release a handful in the water it falls like a shower of sparkling glass. There are perhaps a dozen people here. Four children are collecting shells along the tide-line, and just beyond, a couple of herring gulls are yelling as only herring gulls can, unhinged and ready to burst. We have decided to spend the whole day here. In fact, I'm not going to move from this small patch of sand that I have more or less claimed as mine. When all's said and done, what could be better than this? What else could I want? This is as good as it gets.

And that's the problem, because the moment I have this thought, I have fallen into one of the subtlest of traps. I can acknowledge the richness of God's world, marvel at its almost infinite variety, agree with him in his conversation with Job and say no, I haven't a clue as to how he created any of it, and then, at the moment when I should be lifting my hands in praise and adoration, I run off and enjoy myself. The enticements are varied, and the enticements are good. The earth and all that is in it – loved ones, friends, jobs, hobbies, holidays – provide an almost endless list. These are good things, worthwhile things, and I am sure that our Father wants us to enjoy them. After all, I am sure that he enjoys them. But imagine all these things instead as a love gift, and we have a new perspective.

Children at Christmas and on birthdays are often bombarded with gifts, and their reaction to this can be highly entertaining. There were times when our own children, when very young, would open the present, look at the contents, discard them and then proceed to play for hours with the box. Sometimes they would open the present only to howl with disappointment. At other times they weren't disappointed, but this was simply because they hadn't a clue as to what the gift was, and they sat there in bewilderment, holding it awkwardly as if it might bite. And then there were those moments when our children were so delighted with their presents that they would rush off to play with them without saying a word to anyone. We'd chase after them and insist on a thank you, which, in fairness, they would then say, but it was clear that their priority was elsewhere. Here was something special that had been given to them, and they were going to enjoy it. It had absorbed them fully.

You see the danger. Absorbed in the gift, we ignore the giver. What happens with children on their birthdays happens to us adults on every day of every year. It's possible to spend a lifetime without doing what the psalmist does in Psalm 8, looking at the sky, the moon and the stars and then considering the place of man in it all and the greatness of the God who brought it all into being. But there's more. A gift is only a token of our love; it represents a relationship that we have or that we would like to have. At its heart it represents the one who gives. The real gift is never what it seems. A woman would be foolish to assume that her engagement ring – however much was paid for it – is the whole deal. In fact it is just a pointer to the real gift, which is a relationship with her husband, and then more, her husband himself.

In short, God himself is the gift, and that's hard for children like us who cannot easily see beyond the wrapping paper or the box. For at best these are simply pointers to something much greater; at worst they are an illusion which we can all too easily mistake for the real thing. In saying, "Here is my world for you to enjoy," God is giving a much greater invitation: "Here am I for you to enjoy." The woman who prefers her engagement ring to her husband has missed the point entirely and doesn't have the relationship she may think she has. Not so the psalmist in Psalm 63. These are strong words, reminiscent of the beautiful love-song that is the Song of Solomon.

O God, you are my God,
and I long for you.
My whole being desires you;
like a dry, worn-out, and waterless land,
my soul is thirsty for you.

Do I long for God like this, or do I tuck him into one of my many compartments labelled 'spare-time activities'? Is God the object of my desires or simply an amusement on a Sunday morning? Is my soul hungry and thirsty for him, or is he an afternoon snack that I can just as easily do without? When I let myself dwell on the person of the Lord, do I have all that I desire? God's word teaches us that he will not leave us longing for him without our getting anywhere. In Jeremiah 29:13 God says, "You will seek me, and you will find me, because you will seek me with all your heart."

By way of a test, ask yourself what you think of when you wake up at three o'clock in the morning and can't get back to sleep. I confess that for me this is the most awful time, the time when I most easily give in to worrying and to feeling old. But look at the psalmist: "As I lie in bed, I remember you; all night long I think of you." This is the voice of someone who has fallen in love, and that's the point. Ask yourself if, like him, you are sitting in the shadow of God's wings, singing for joy. And if you aren't, then where are you? And what are you doing?

44

IN THE NIGHT

Each night, as darkness
Sucks blood from a sleeping world,
My thoughts turn to God.

Delicate, the moon
Peels back the flesh of my heart,
Awakes my longing.

Six feet from my face
Stars, suspended on thin wires,
Unravel meaning,

Dissect my life's work,
Push pieces to the plate's edge:
Discarded fish bones.

Thin as a bat's wing,
The shell of what I was falls
Upward into space.

There is only God.
Pin-prick sensitive, I am
Wrapped tight in his arms

And held, like a child,
Fast, close-bodied, until I
Waken to a dream.

A Prayer

Forgive me, Father,
When I have made,
And when I still make, gods
Of all that is not you.
Forgive me, Father,
When I have bowed before objects,
Places, people, created things,
As if they had created me, as if they were
My source of life, and that is only you.
And help me, Father, in the night,
When fear looms and fills my mind
With thoughts of losing all I cherish,
And of losing life itself; when I forget that life
Does bring death, but that, in Christ,
My death brings life eternal.

7

Holy Ground

Joshua 5:13-15; 6:1-27

THE BOOK OF JOSHUA IS A BOOK ABOUT MEN OF ACTION, A book of brave and heroic deeds. It's a book of adventure, capture and conquest, a book in which God at last fulfils the promises made long before to Moses and brings his people home. And who is leading these people? Joshua, straight and direct, upright and honest, committed and faithful. In his old age, addressing the people and reviewing the workings of God among them, he urges them to turn their backs on foreign gods and choose God alone. Then he says, simply and beautifully, "As for my family and me, we will serve the Lord," meaning, I think, "even if we are the only ones who do". [Josh.24:14-15]

Although I love being caught up in the action of this book, the part which stirs me most is the passage at the end of Joshua 5. It's sandwiched between the dramatic and miraculous crossing of the Jordan, mirroring that of the Red Sea, and the equally dramatic and miraculous fall of Jericho. There's another mirror image here too, of course. Joshua's encounter with the angel of the Lord recalls Moses' meeting with God early in the book of Exodus, and but for the perhaps arbitrary division of chapters, they follow a very similar sequence. However, during a recent reading of Joshua, this division of the chapters became all important to me.

In Exodus chapter 3 Moses is distracted from his shepherding by the unusual sight of a burning bush which does not burn away. As he approaches, God says to him, "Do not come any closer. Take off your sandals, because you are standing on holy ground. I am the God of your ancestors, the God of Abraham, Isaac, and Jacob." Then, in the space of no more than a verse, the passage continues with God's explanation of what this meeting is about, the freeing of the Israelites from Egypt, and we are immediately caught up in that business, just as Moses was.

Joshua's encounter is similar. Unexpectedly he sees a man holding a sword, and although at first there is uncertainty as to his identity, the mystery doesn't last long. Joshua too has to take off his shoes for he, like Moses, is standing on holy ground. And as in Exodus, there follows a list of instructions, this time concerning the destruction of Jericho. But these are in chapter 6. If you carry on reading, it might as well be all the same chapter. But if, as I was doing recently, you are reading one chapter at a time, the story becomes very different. This time, and quite unlike the Moses story, I did not press on with the adventure. I didn't do what we all want to do: find out what happens next.

I was made to stop. Artificially, perhaps, but I stopped just as Joshua did. And just like Joshua, I'd come to expect a list of instructions, but there was only one: take off your shoes. Here is a simple but profound truth. The Jordan had been crossed, and Jericho would fall, but here, in between these two unforgettable events, is something more important: Joshua alone with his God. No instructions; not even any words. A time of stillness in the presence of God. A time of adoration. A time of worship.

Take off your shoes, for this is holy ground. When we meet God we have no right to anything that is of ourselves, and we meet on his terms, not ours. God invites us and takes pleasure in our presence, but he is holy, completely other. The only attitude available to us is that of bowing down and worshipping. God is not our 'mate'. We come to him in awe, wonder and humility, and we must deny all that is of ourselves, or we miss the point. The essence of worship is that we are caught up in God, not that God is caught up in us. For worship to be real, we must lose ourselves in him. Then, when we have nothing left of ourselves, God can give himself to us, so that recreated in him we can be the people we were, and are, meant to be.

Now, here's the point. What happens when God outlines his plans to Moses? Moses argues, says he can't do it and asks God to find someone else. And perhaps it's unfair to compare the exodus from Egypt with the fall of Jericho, but look at chapter 6. When the instructions come to Joshua, and they do, you and I don't hear what Joshua hears, because we know how the story ends. What Joshua hears is a list of commands that make no sense at all. How many cities have fallen just because an army has walked around them, and because priests have blown trumpets and people have shouted? We don't think about how weird these things are, because we know they worked. But what did Joshua think? Did he imagine the people of Jericho looking down from their walls and laughing at this ridiculous charade? Did he imagine day seven, when all the Israelites shouted their heads off and nothing happened, when decades in the desert had resulted only in a shameful disaster?

We don't know, but probably not. There's a clue in chapter 5, verse 15. When Joshua was told to take off his shoes, he "did as he was told". In his encounter with God, Joshua allowed God to be God. Joshua was an extraordinary man, certainly, but he'd met an extraordinary God. He had discovered, barefoot on this holy ground, just who this God was with his flashing sword, and he knew that the fall of Jericho lay not in his own hands – never would and never could – but in the hands of a God who would bring glory to himself and who would do it in whichever way suited him best.

I am reminded of 2 Chronicles 20, where King Jehoshaphat is up against the armies of Moab and Ammon. In their dread, the king and his people come together to pray. They worship God, humble themselves and ask for his help. Then the Spirit of the Lord comes upon a Levite who prophesies, "The Lord says that you must not be discouraged or be afraid to face this large army. The battle depends on God, not on you." I am encouraged too by versions which have Joshua 6:2 as, "See, *I have delivered* Jericho into your hands…" For people like you and me, victims of linear time, the battle lies ahead and is still a frightening prospect. Not so for God, for whom time past and time future are one and the same, so that the thing that God has decreed must happen has, in effect, already happened. "Don't be afraid of the people of Jericho," says God. " *You have already beaten them.*"

And you, you to whom the secrets of the kingdom of heaven have been revealed, do you take off your shoes and kneel before God on holy ground? Are the walls of Jericho standing high above you? Are its citizens staring down at you, strong and confident in their security? Do you not know how to lead your people? Are the risks too great? Are you afraid? Well, you know what to do.

If this Christian life of ours is going to go in the direction that God intends, then at its very heart must be our worship of him. Perhaps we need to do this more often than we think. Perhaps we need to do it differently. What I sense is that we need to take off our shoes and come and stand on holy ground. And we need to pray that God will raise up among us those who will teach us how to worship him. We might have some learning to do, but that's all right. Why would we ever think that we've arrived, when there might be a burning bush or an angel holding a flashing sword just around the next corner?

Armistice

11TH NOVEMBER, 2019

It was an act of remembrance,
Standing quiet
At eleven in the morning
In a supermarket aisle,
Alongside other shoppers,
Shelf-stackers,
Sales assistants, each one
Somebody else remembering,
Each one
Perhaps remembering somebody else,
As I was,
Standing quiet
In that supermarket aisle
For two minutes,
The silence taking on
For two minutes
A palpable stillness
Shared warmly
In wordless community.
And then, so quickly,
The music again
And bodies as though reviving,
Checking prices,
Dropping items
Casually,
Maybe thoughtlessly,
Into plastic baskets,
And me
Who would have preferred not to move,
As if in the space
Of only two minutes
I had glimpsed something other-worldly
In this unexpected, ordinary place
Where I might have stayed
A little longer,
Where we had become

A little nobler,
Grown together
In this silent act of grieving.

A PRAYER

Lord, I am weak.
But you are strong,
And your strength is made perfect
In my weakness.

I am disloyal.
I have spread my allegiances
Before a thousand lesser gods
Which have crumbled
In a moment at my touch.
But you are faithful.
You refuse to go away when I spit at you;
You refuse to stay at arm's length
When I cry out for you.

I am unforgiving.
From my moral high ground
I am the king of everything I see.
But you are merciful.
Seventy times seven times
You multiply forgiveness
In your hands
Like loaves and fishes.

I am afraid
When you choose to use my hands
As if they were your own.
And you promise me your way,
Your truth, your life,
As if they were sufficient.

I am not an optimist,
But with the passing of each night
A new dawn creeps hesitant above the hills,
And you must think
The world is worth another day.
And so I follow you,

Bound in love,
A prisoner of hope.

8

Mighty Warriors

Judges 6

I WONDER HOW WELL YOU KNOW YOURSELF, HOW WELL you know what sort of a person you are. It's important to know our strengths and weaknesses, the ways in which we're tempted, the rhythms to which we tick. Such knowledge is valuable and works towards our spiritual maturity, but it only goes so far. For one thing, we all know people who overestimate their strengths, and we're equally familiar with those who overestimate their weaknesses. Let's be honest, the church has no shortage of either. But it's not really them and us, is it? The truth is that as we get older we discover that we never fully come to know ourselves. We are, very often, a storm of emotions, moods and motives which we cannot come close to mastering and which are a constant source of amazement to us. St Paul said he did the things he didn't want to do and didn't do the things he wanted to do. [Rom.7:15] We're the same. Each year we make our New Year's resolutions, but we usually make them flippantly and we often make the wrong ones. No wonder we rarely keep them. In response to the ancient saying "Know thyself", we can only say, "I can't." I am my own best friend and my own worst enemy, and although it's a cliché, there is some truth in the familiar lament, "I don't know who I am any more."

So it's just as well that God does, because it is in him and not in ourselves that we find our identity. In fact we shouldn't bother looking anywhere else, because nobody knows us like he does, and what he knows about us is much truer than anything that our self-centred fumbling might come up with. After all, "You created every part of me; you put me together in my mother's womb." [Ps.139:13] We rarely come close to seeing ourselves as God sees us, and Gideon is no exception. Despite what Gideon may think, the angel isn't joking when he addresses him with the words "Brave and mighty man!" In God's eyes, that's what Gideon is, because in the strength of God that's what he will prove himself to be. Perhaps, like Gideon, you thought it was sarcasm. Perhaps, if the angel of the Lord had said this to you, you would have replied with the line I once heard in a children's play, "If I'm such a brave and mighty man, why am I hiding in this winepress?"

Gideon's actual response isn't much different: if God is with us, why are we in such a mess? And they really are in a mess, but God is going to get them out of it. It's worth following the story closely, because the development of Gideon's faith in his God is interesting. Even after miraculous signs of God's power and Gideon's destruction of the pagan altar, Gideon still puts out his famous fleeces. God is patient with him and humours him, but when all that is finished, and when Gideon has been brought to a point when he just might believe that God really is in all this, God plays his trump card and removes most of the soldiers. God's intention is plain: if I leave a great number of men, they will think they have won the battle on their own.

This is the big irony about God's mighty men: they let God do the fighting. It's not that they are cowards. Going into battle knowing that by yourself you are not up to it takes a lot of courage, but this courage isn't based on a belief in yourself but on a belief in the God who fights on your behalf. Gideon's real battle is coming to that point of faith where he can believe that God is who he says he is, so he proves himself to be a brave and mighty man twice over: firstly for being prepared to confront the enemy, and secondly, and more importantly, for stepping out of his hiding place and trusting that God will do what he has said he will do. So it is that in God, Gideon becomes the person that God has already seen him to be.

The Bible tells us repeatedly who we are in God, but we're slow to learn. We find it hard to believe such good things about ourselves. Recently a friend went for prayer ministry suffering from a stiff neck and headaches. The couple ministering prayed for his healing and then, as is often done, simply remained still before the Lord. After a short while, one of them said to our friend, "The Lord wants you to know that in him you are a strong man." Just like that, not expected and not asked for, but important for somebody who saw himself as anything but strong. God was saying, "That's how you see yourself; now I'll tell you how I see you. Let's exchange your reality for mine, your untruth for my truth. In me, this is who you are." Our friend went up with a headache and came away with an identity.

In a previous church there were many beautiful and helpful banners on display. One of my favourites was based on texts in Deuteronomy, Psalms and Zechariah and said simply, "You are the apple of my eye."

Life throws up all sorts of reasons for forgetting that this is true, so this was a good reminder week by week of how God feels about us. It was an antidote to my own often less edifying thoughts and feelings about who I am. The Bible never tries to kid us about our identity, and neither does it hide it from us: I am a child of God, I am a friend of Jesus and I am a citizen of heaven. It's a good idea, I think, when we come across such bold, life-affirming statements from God to write them down and reflect on them, especially in our gloomier moments. God's picture of us is invariably fuller and more beautiful than the picture we have of ourselves. When Jesus says that Peter is the Rock, I doubt if that's how Peter sees himself, but the Rock is what he becomes. In God I am always much more than I am in myself, and if I allow it, I can become the person he sees me to be. Because in him I already am.

We can help each other in this, too, and that's good because it's so easy to feel down in the dumps about who we are. Most of us know that we won't compete in the next Olympics, but even in the family of the church it isn't hard to have a sense of being worth very little. Once, during a home group course, we did an exercise. Pieces of paper were given out, each one having the name of one person in the group. Then we thought about why we valued each other. This might have been about skills or abilities, but I was hoping we would concentrate more on what sort of people we were and on why we valued each other. Having finished, we passed on each sheet and wrote about the next person. After about fifteen minutes the sheets were complete, and with each person's permission we read them out. You might think that this sounds pretty cheesy, but in fact it was one of the most moving things we had done in home group. People were genuinely touched, and I'm sure it was because for some of them this was the first time they had felt appreciated, not simply for what they did but also for who they were.

Perhaps in your church you encourage each other all the time. Perhaps you don't. We decided that evening that it was a habit we should get into, though I admit that so far I have only had limited success. Like a lot more things that are worth doing, you have to work at it. All I know is that if encouragement has the effect I saw it have that evening, the church would be a different place if we practised it more often. So have a go. Encourage somebody. Pluck up the courage to thank someone for their contribution to this or that, praise them for a task well done, express appreciation for who they are, or even let them know that they are a mighty warrior for the Lord. We are, after all, family, so let's build each other up, because in that we will come to understand more fully who we are, not simply in the body of Christ, or even in Christ's army, but in Christ himself.

RUNNING

I do forget, sometimes,
That I am not alone in this.
I forget the weight that always is
Attached to nationhood and tribe,
To clan and family.
Like it or not, I am a part of each;
Countless specks of sand make up one beach.
I do forget, sometimes,
That a voice which purrs inside my head
Suggestions that I take a different course,
Make one or two short cuts,
And please myself a little more
Is not always my own voice,
Though it may sound for all the world like me.
I forget, sometimes, that God is in this too;
That he runs, is always running
Down that twisting road with arms wide;
That he pulls me back indoors,
Says, "Everything I have is yours."
And I do forget the crowd,
Some glued trackside, some with the blue sky
Wrapped like a wave around their broad shoulders,
Cheering, and shouting encouragement
To one among all others in a race,
A boy with a stone in his shoe
And uncertainty scratched in lines across his face,
Who wishes, as his legs that are no longer
Part of him begin to tire,
That this crowd, drifting away in his dull ears,
Would raise their voice a little higher.

We underestimate, I think, the importance and the power of blessing. Here is an expanded version of Psalm 23, and my prayer suggestion is as follows. Firstly, pray the blessing over yourself, replacing the "your" with "my" etc. And secondly, bless someone else with it, reading it aloud and saying their name before each verse. The Lord encourages us to bless each other, and he will bless the other person as you do, only more.

A Prayer with a Blessing

May the Lord be your shepherd,
Your own shepherd, yours.
May he snatch you from the snapping jaws
Of the lion, out from its sharpened claws,
Carry you home,
Bring you safely indoors.

May the Lord be your Good Shepherd,
Leave his ninety-nine penned sheep,
Snug and blanketed by a log fire,
To go out in search of you,
Hopelessly lost,
Bramble-tangled and bleating
In that place where the cloud sits like death
On the side of the hill,
And where you're needing, more than anything,
A saviour.

May the Lord give you everything you need.
May he give you the wisdom to know what you need
And desire enough to ask for it.
May he open the doors of his heavenly storehouses
And pour out blessing
To fall like silver snow
Upon your grateful head.

May the Lord lead you into lush green water meadows
And picnic with you beside quiet streams.
May the days stretch out for you,
A moment becoming an hour;
And there, in the still, mayfly-dancing air,

May your flagging spirits be restored,
And may you know peace.

May the Lord walk by your side
In the light and in the darkness,
When you're up and when you're down,
In gladness and in fear.
And when your path under high cliffs
Lies deep in shadow,
May the Lord be your travelling companion,
Hold your hand when you need it,
Weep with you a little,
Laugh with you a lot more,
And lead you, always, to a place
Where there is so much more light
Than there ever was before.

May the Lord welcome you into his presence
And treat you as his special guest.
May he prepare a banquet for you,
And may your table groan
Under the weight of the choicest food.
May the Lord save the best wine until last,
Vindicate you before those who have done you harm
Or spoken ill of you;
And may he give you the grace to finish well
The race that you have begun.

Then, when you have tasted his goodness
And his mercy all your life,
May you go to live with him
In that place that he has gone ahead
To prepare for you.
May you see your Good Shepherd
Face to face,
And know him, just as you yourself are known.

9

Keeping Still

Exodus 14

BECAUSE WE KNOW HOW THE STORY ENDED, WE TEND NOT
to think too much about what it must have felt like to be in the middle
of it, trying to escape from Egypt while being hunted down by
Pharaoh's armies. The Israelites didn't know the outcome as we now
do. They judged only by what they were experiencing at the time, and
what they were experiencing wasn't good.

The Israelites were afraid, and they were panicking. They feared at
best a return to slavery, at worst an unpleasant death there in the desert.
And so they wished they had stayed put in Egypt, where at least they
might have lived a little longer and where they might have died a little
less unpleasantly. So, here's the question: what were they thinking of
doing now? Were they thinking of fighting? Not much chance of
success there. Were they thinking of running away? Very little chance
there either, with the sea on one side and the Egyptians on the other.
Truth is, there wasn't much they *could* do. Except grumble, of course.
They were pretty good at that.

As always, God takes a different approach, and he tells them to do
two things that they wouldn't have thought of doing in a million years.
There they are in verse 14. Number one: Trust me to fight for you. This
was hard. After all, the Lord hadn't fought for them before, so why
should he start now? But hang on, who was it that had sent the plagues
upon the Egyptians? Who was it that had killed the firstborn? Who was
it that had brought them miraculously out of Egypt? And who was it
that had sent Moses to them, without whom they would still be hauling
bricks and dying a slow death?

Number two: Be still. There are many different versions of the
second part of this verse: be still; stay calm; be silent; hold your peace;
there is no need for you to do anything. Any one is good. Put together
they are even better, though it's still a difficult instruction, because by
nature we all want to do something, control things, make an effort, and
believe not just that sorting things out is our responsibility but that if

61

we don't do it, nobody else will. So we look around frantically for a solution to our problem, and when we can't find one we do the only thing that we have left; we take it out on anybody who happens to be around, particularly if that somebody is supposed to be in charge.

Our logic goes like this: we have nobody to help us, so we are on our own (like we always knew we were!), but there is nothing we can do, so it's hopeless. God's logic is different: I have fought for you before, because I love you and hold you close to my heart, so you can sit back and allow me to fight for you again. In other words, he invites us to be still and to know that he is God.

And then the impossible happens. God devises – had always devised – a way of escape that we wouldn't have come up with if we'd had a lifetime to think about it. And even if we had come up with it, it was a solution that we would never have been able to bring about by ourselves. Not ever. For God it was such a small thing, but it was completely beyond us, just as God is completely beyond us. Isn't it fortunate for us, then, that in Jesus he has chosen not to be?

JESUS IN THE CASTLE AT MARVÃO

All he does is sit there in the shade, waiting,
Hands in his lap, legs folded,
Not moving, just waiting,
Eyes looking out over castle walls
Where the rock thrush sings,
Out over rosebushes and neat hedges,
As if to some no man's land
That is neither Portugal nor Spain,
Neither earth nor sky,
Neither here nor there,
Horizons melting into haze,
A blue translucent film
That's thin enough
To push your finger through.

I, on the other hand, can't sit
And spoil my visit.
I have to make a circuit of the walls,
Mark out in the stretching landscape
Where we've come from,
Where we're going next.
I'll try to photograph the thrush
If he'll keep still,
And snap the lipstick-red geraniums
On whitewashed houses, eye-blinding
In this sun that falls on my head like stones.
"Look for my heart," says Jesus,
As if it were that easy,
My eye caught now by cardinal fritillaries,
Frantic in olive and orange,
Twitching nervously on purple thistles
And, to my frustration,
Not wanting to settle for even one moment.

A Prayer

Lord,
At times I think you must be playing games with me,
Setting me up for a fall,
Bringing me to stand between rocks and hard places,
Letting me know how Moses felt, on that shore
With tens of thousands, but alone
Between the devil and the deep blue sea.
And yet I've known you long enough to know
You are sufficient, that you have no limits,
That nothing is impossible for you.
I've known you long enough to know
That when I'm seeing no way out, you're waiting,
Waiting for me to wait, waiting for me
To come to an end in myself,
To be still before you, and to know that you are God.

10

For Times Like This

Esther 4

OUR THREE CHILDREN, NOW GROWN, MARRIED AND WITH children of their own, live within fifty miles of us but in opposite directions. This means that whilst we see each of them quite often, it's much less frequent that we all meet up together. So when another big family gathering was announced, we jumped at the chance, and we looked forward to it. On this occasion it was to be at our son's, and we did what we often do; we decided to stretch out the day and fit in another visit on our way, this time a little detour to see Small Blue butterflies on the Mendip Hills. This was a mistake, for two reasons.

The first reason is that we didn't see any Small Blues, but we had seen them on previous occasions so we quickly got over our disappointment. The second reason is that on returning to our car we saw a long, wet snake running down the hill and we realised that our car was in trouble. Knowing nothing whatsoever about engines, but knowing that if I called the breakdown people we would almost certainly be very late arriving at our destination, I decided to fill up with water and hope for the best.

This was another mistake, because a couple of miles further on I had to fill up again, and then again a few miles later. After two further fill-ups, and down to the cartons of fruit juice we were taking to our son's, we decided that enough was enough and we turned into a side road and made the phone call that I had been reluctant to make earlier. We were there two hours.

But two things happened in this place where we had so randomly stopped which almost certainly wouldn't have happened had we ended up anywhere else. The first concerned the loud music that was coming from a garden next to where we had parked. I need to tell you here that loud music played in gardens is close to the top of my hate list, and here I was, being forced to listen to it. I couldn't close the car windows; it was too warm. I couldn't move the car; I'd given precise instructions to the AA. I couldn't be wonderfully calm; I dislike it that much. So what was I to do and think and feel when, having discovered our predicament, the owners of the music brought us tea and biscuits on a tray and then, seeing our need, invited us into their house to use their facilities? What was I to do and think and feel when these people I didn't know and would probably never meet again treated us with the sort of kindness that Jesus loves and encourages, when all the while I had been having such uncharitable thoughts about them and their music? I know the answer, so please don't tell me.

The other thing was even less likely. There was a church nearby, and we got talking to an elderly lady who had been opening up the church hall for some people who had hired it. It turned out that her brother was very unwell, on the point of death in fact, but for reasons I don't remember she had been unable to go to see him and she was now waiting for the inevitable phone call. So here was something very improbable: while I, at the mechanic's instruction, was revving the engine like mad and making more noise than a dozen radios put together, Carol was sitting in a garden talking and praying with a complete stranger and blessing her with the peace of God. The Lord cracks me up sometimes, he really does. And if you're wondering how it all ended, we arrived very late, of course, but our lovely family had saved us two big platefuls of food (in my very fragile emotional state, twelve baskets would have killed me), and when in the early evening we set off for home, we didn't feel that we had missed out in any way. I'm not saying that the sun had stood still, but the day had been long enough for it all.

Now, I'm not claiming for a moment that I understand fully, or perhaps even partly, what was going on here. I'm not saying, for example, that the Lord deliberately punctured our coolant hose or that he wilfully deprived our children of their parents' wonderful company. I'm simply suggesting that for me it was a very memorable example of what we find in Romans 8:28: "We know that in all things God works for good with those who love him." I can just imagine the Lord that morning saying to himself, "One of my children is going to need some comforting today. Let's see who I've got in her area." A bit like the AA, I suppose.

For me the story of Esther is about just that. Haman, mastermind of the imminent destruction of all Jews in the Persian Empire, instructs the magicians and astrologers to cast lots to determine the most favourable day for this planned destruction. Unusually for books of the Bible, God and his plans are nowhere mentioned. Events are set in motion and, it seems, kept moving by only two things, the schemes of men and sheer randomness, rather like our day out in the car. But it's an illusion, because again I can imagine the Lord looking on, this time saying to himself, "My people are about to be killed. I wonder who I have in the area." Mordecai is spot on in his message to Esther: "Yet who knows – maybe it was for a time like this that you were made queen!"

But if that's true, then the Lord has been working all along, because Esther didn't become queen overnight; her position and her character were a long time in the making. So the Lord is right in there, in among all the plots of men and the apparent randomness of everything, bringing good out of evil, transforming it, redeeming it and, if we let him, using us to bring about his purposes. Esther didn't have to let him, but she did. We don't have to let him either. If we don't, he'll find somebody else, but he'd rather it was us. Chances are, we're his first choice.

On reflection I was pleased that the Lord had used us in this way, but I would rather he'd said to me over breakfast, "Look John, you're going to have trouble with the car today. Don't be alarmed when this happens; just park up in the spot I'm showing you in this vision you're now having. I need you both to be in that place, and when you get there I'll show you what to do." Instead, I had to learn the lesson more or less in reverse, looking back and seeing how the Lord had worked. I can't help wondering if over each day's breakfast I should try to get into the habit of imagining him saying something similar: "Look John, not everything today will be plain sailing, but if things become a bit rocky, remember that I'm in it all with you. So stay calm, and don't be afraid, because I will bring you through it. And try to stay open to my opportunities, because if you're willing I'd like to use you to bring blessing to others." Maybe from the Lord's point of view that's a typical day. The question is, would I like it to be a typical day for me too?

SLOW AND STEADY

I know
I go
Too slow
For you.
You walk and leap
For God,
I only plod.
Two forward steps,
Then three reverse;
A few good days
Are followed by
A week that's worse.
I'd love to race ahead,
Then turn and wave,
Shout, "It's all right out here,
It's safe,
No need to fear."
But
I lack the confidence
To run;
Maybe I'll fall.
It isn't unbelief at all,
More a preference for
Slow and steady;
I overdose on
Getting ready.
I have always been the same:
Afraid of moving
To an outside lane,
Fearful, perhaps,
That in the glare of sunlight
And the open air
The Lord might call my name,
Might want me there.

A Prayer at the Start of the Day

Lord,

You have given me this new day, which now I offer, with all that is in it, back to you. It is your gift to me, and it is my gift to you.

I ask that through every hour you keep me from anger and despair, and that you fill me instead with joy and hope.

May I at each encounter bless and not curse, build up and not tear down.

May I in each moment see an opportunity to be a channel of your grace.

May I see each person as a child of God waiting to meet Jesus in me.

In my thinking, in my speaking and in my doing, may I bring honour to you, my Lord and Saviour.

11

Guard the Anointing

Judges 13-16

SOMETHING I'VE UNDERSTOOD WITH AGE IS JUST HOW much our perceptions change along with our perspectives. Many of us will have heard the comment that is generally, though apparently incorrectly, attributed to Mark Twain, that when he was eighteen he thought his father was pretty dumb, but when he reached twenty-one he was amazed by how much the old man had learned in only three years. It happens to all of us in one way or another. I remember that when I first read Flaubert's *Madame Bovary*, aged seventeen, I thought what a very sad tale it was. Reading it again a few years later, I couldn't believe how funny it had become in so short a time. A similar thing happened with my approach to the life of King David. As a boy, I responded primarily to his heroic deeds and great exploits, whereas later on I was struck much more forcibly by the very sizeable mess he got himself into.

The same is true of Samson, whom I used to see as the Old Testament equivalent of the Incredible Hulk, that's to say as a wonderful superhero. Now though, whilst I wouldn't want to take anything away from his feats of strength or from his part in the Israelite struggle against the Philistines, I find my attention drawn to his less than heroic side and to the very important message that I think shouts out from it. I say *I think*, because I'm pretty sure that if asked, very many people would say, probably thanks to art, opera, film, popular music and whatever else, that Samson's principal weakness was his inability to resist a pretty woman. That's part of it, of course, but as I've reflected on his story it seems to me that far more important than that, because it spans all his failings, is Samson's refusal to take his calling seriously. It's not a story about Samson and Delilah, as the world would have us believe. It's a story about Samson and God, or at least that's what it was meant to be.

I wonder, if you'd been asked to list those special people in the Bible whose birth is announced with an angelic visitation, whether or not you would have included Samson. But that's what happens, because he's that special, and not just special but set apart and dedicated to God. [Jdg.13:5-7; Num.6:8] Sadly, and this determines the pattern of his adult life, Samson hasn't read the terms and conditions, or if he has, he's ignoring them. The angel couldn't have been clearer about the Nazirite regulations, and Samson can't be unaware of them, but he continually disregards them, preferring instead to do his own thing. Even his hair, the source of his strength, he trades in for a bit of peace and quiet from his deceitful girlfriend. And he has had plenty of warning that this was the way things were heading.

Samson's first recorded act as an adult is to meet a Philistine girl and demand that his parents arrange the wedding. There's so much that's wrong here. Among other things, what about God's instruction not to marry into the nations who worshipped other gods? And what about the commandment about honouring your father and your mother? But treating his parents as servants, the spoiled child gets his way, and from now on his way will be that of living by his own rules, the way of self-reliance and self-belief in the worst sense of those words. He isn't led by the Lord, and he appears not to seek guidance. Instead, he simply reacts, both to personal affront and to difficult situations, situations that he often has a big part in creating. Thinking himself invincible, he comes to believe that he will be able to get himself out of whatever scrape he's got himself into. It's a belief that says, "God is on *my* side, what could possibly go wrong?" And if that's true, then it doesn't really matter how he lives or what he does. He can keep a foot in both camps. He can have his cake and eat it, because, "I'll get loose and go free as always." He'll live each day trusting in himself and in the gift which the Lord has given him, until, perhaps inevitably, that day comes when he tosses away the gift as if it has no value, at which point the giver of the gift gently takes his leave too.

None of this is to say that the Lord doesn't use Samson. He does, of course, and the Philistines are very much worse off for Samson's being around. But when we read that "Samson killed more people at his death than he had killed during his life", I don't take this as a justification for the way he has lived that life. Just the opposite. I think it's saying that the Lord has used Samson to great effect despite Samson, and it's also asking us to consider what might have been had Samson lived a life of obedience to the call, humbling himself as a servant of the Lord rather than living as if he were the one in charge. What might the Lord say right now about Samson? Perhaps something like, "I loved

Samson very much, and I had great plans for him, but he wasn't having any of it."

In case you think I'm being too critical of Samson, and he is after all included in the great list of the faithful in Hebrews 11, what I'm trying to do more than anything is to sound a warning, because it is so very easy for us not to take our calling seriously. You might think otherwise. You might think that nobody in their right mind, having received a calling from the God of heaven, would ever jeopardise both the calling and themselves by treating it casually, by giving as much weight to it as if it were nothing more than a free gift in a packet of cereals. But it happens, and you know it happens. Only last week I heard of another church leader who had had to step down over some ill-judged behaviour, and before we get high and mighty over that, I'll say now that it could just as easily have been me. Or perhaps you.

So, guard your anointing. Take your calling seriously. And I don't mean simply the calling you have to a particular ministry, though I include that. I mean that special relationship that you have as a child of God, indwelt and gifted by the same Spirit who gifted Samson. Because the temptation is always there to treat it very casually, to do everything in our own way, to keep a foot in every camp we come across, and then to trade in our birthright for nothing more than a bowl of hot stew.

And if you don't do it already, please pray for your leaders. Don't assume that simply because God has chosen them to be leaders they have a greater inbuilt armour against temptation. They don't. In fact it's more likely that as leaders they are facing greater temptation. So pray for them. Who knows, your prayers may make all the difference between your leaders going off the rails and their being the best leaders your church has ever had. One day the Lord will take you to one side and say, "Well done!" You'll ask, "For what?" And he'll remind you of all those times you prayed for your leaders. "Oh," you'll say, "I'd forgotten that." And he'll say, "Well, I haven't, and it made all the difference."

MORNING PRAYERS

At that far too early hour
Before the sun itself
Has struggled to rise,
When sleeping children stretch out
Like starfish on white sheets
And parents turn a blind eye
To the coming day...
At that far too early hour
Jesus wakes,
And makes his way
Through cold, unpeopled streets to pray,
Alone, out where it's wild,
Feet hanging
Over some precipitous ravine,
Hands smelling
Of crushed herbs, and turned
Outwards
And upwards to his Father.
"Come, Holy Spirit," are his only words,
And then a slow release of breath,
Hands falling gently,
Palms still open,
Till they rest upon his knees,
Tears running
Unbidden
And unhindered down his cheeks.

A Prayer

Father, forgive me,
When you have opened up your way to me,
And I have wandered from it, carelessly;
Father, forgive me,
When you have shown your heart's desires to me,
And I have chased my eyes' desires, stubbornly;
Father, forgive me,
When you have made plain your will to me,
And I have countered, proudly, with my own.
It seems that there is nothing good in me.
But you have laid my sin on Jesus,
And you are jealous for my heart;
So help me, Lord, each day,
To guard my heart,
To walk as Jesus walks,
To desire as he desires,
And to will as he wills.
Help me, at all times and in all places,
To guard my anointing,
That your promise may be made full in me,
To your honour and to your great pleasure.

12

Think on These Things

2 Samuel 11

WE'VE JUST HAD OUR GRAND-DAUGHTERS TO STAY FOR the weekend. It's been the pleasure that it always is, and I was again amused by their first words on arriving, which were, as they almost always are, "What are we going to make today, Granny?" Grandad, you understand, helps them with their homework, whereas Granny has that perhaps more enviable, if more exhausting job: she makes things with them. And so it is that when the girls say goodbye, they leave laden down with cakes, biscuits, pictures, toilet-roll sculptures and much more besides, none of which had existed – hadn't been much thought about – before they arrived. And then, when we've tidied, hoovered and flopped down into armchairs, we reflect once again on just how wonderful it has been, not simply to spend time with them but also to see the creative spirit so energetically in action.

Of course, it all starts with our heavenly Father, the ultimate creator, ever imaginative, ever inventive and eternally unstoppable. In whatever way the world was formed, God imagined it, created it, moulded it and made it, too, unstoppable. Imagination and desire, creative impulse, the word, the event. "'Let there be light,'" says God, "and light appeared." [Gen.1:3] We are first formed in the mind of the Creator, in his imagination, and then we are brought forth.

Man too, having been imagined and created in God's image, imagines and creates. Houses, for example, do not happen by accident, even if we tend to grumble that they are "springing up everywhere". Houses are seen in the imagination long before the first concrete is poured. There are plans and more plans, and then plans that are changed as minds are changed along the way. And then, if things go *according to plan*, there comes that gentle exhalation of breath as we say, "It's exactly as I pictured it," or better still, "It's even more beautiful than I had imagined." Houses are built first in the mind. This is the way things work. It's the way we work. It's the way God works.

And that's fine while we are imagining and creating things that are good, or at worst morally neutral. Unfortunately, in our tendency towards evil, we can give our imaginations a certain liberty, even free rein, in areas that are neither good nor morally neutral. It doesn't appear to matter that Jesus doesn't let us get away with that. For example, he says, "...anyone who looks at a woman and wants to possess her is guilty of committing adultery with her in his heart." [Matt.5:28] But men still do it, perhaps excusing themselves with the notion that as this is merely imagined, it isn't real. Jesus is saying the opposite: it *is* real. In God's reality, which is the only true reality, what we do on the inside is every bit as important and every bit as real as what we do on the outside.

There's worse to come, because as we've seen, the act begins in the imagination. It follows that it is more likely that we will fall into sin if we have given ourselves over to imagining the sin beforehand. Whatever the temptation is, it will be more difficult to resist if in our minds we have become experts at giving in to it. If that's the case, then when the 'real life' temptation comes along, we may find ourselves leaping into the tempter's arms. After all, we have in effect been planning this for a long time, although, unlike our dream house, it will not turn out to be better than we had pictured in our imagination. Or not for long. It is important, therefore, to do all we can not to allow the enemy a foothold. Too many footholds become a stronghold, and at that point we are giving control to another. Put like that, it is very clearly not what we really want.

It was the spring, and if King David had led his troops off to war as he should have done, the sorry tale that was about to unfold would have been neither imagined nor enacted. As it was, he stayed at home with far too much time on his hands, and as he wandered lazily around the palace roofs his imagination wandered around too, just about everywhere and far more actively. The signposts were as plain as day, especially the one written in bright dayglow capital letters that said, "She's the wife of Uriah the Hittite!" This should have hit him in the face and knocked him out cold, but he appears not to have noticed and sends for her immediately, fuelled by that powerful cocktail of pride, desire and the dizzying sweetness of the imagination.

Inevitably, of course, the events which follow are not one of them what David might previously have imagined. He hadn't imagined that Bathsheba would become pregnant. He hadn't imagined that Uriah would refuse to go home to surely the most desirable woman in

Jerusalem. He hadn't imagined that Uriah would continue to refuse even when drunk on the best wine in the kingdom. He hadn't imagined that one day he, the king, would be giving instructions – hand-delivered by the poor man himself – that would ensure the death of one of the most famous soldiers in the land, one of the thirty, a national hero. And he hadn't imagined all the trouble that would follow on from that – and there really was a lot of trouble still to come. In fact, in this entire sequence of events, David never uses his imagination in any way that we might approve of. Instead, having helped lead him into sin, his imagination now helps him to lie, to deceive, to scheme and to plot. It helps to bring him down, and it's no wonder that the chapter ends with what I consider to be one of the most chilling sentences in the Bible, if only on account of the enormity of its understatement: "But the Lord was not pleased with what David had done."

It seems to me that James sums this up well when he writes, "Then their evil desires conceive and give birth to sin; and sin, when it is full-grown, gives birth to death." [Jas.1:15] It's in the mind where these things start, and if we are not wanting to see in our own lives, even on a much smaller scale, the sort of events that King David saw in his, then it is first in our minds that we need to keep things under control. It was over precisely this matter that a friend of mine spent some time in prayer recently. He told me afterwards that the bulk of his prayer had been a confession of his weakness to the Lord, and then he told me what he sensed God saying to him: "Yes, you are weak, but you're no weaker than anybody else, and you're stronger than many. The real question is not whether you're weak or strong, but whether you're prepared to take a stand, and that stand needs to begin in your thoughts."

That might sound a bit harsh, but it's true, isn't it? Whilst we may want to wallow in our supposed victim status and complain, as we so often do, that it was all Eve's fault, the Lord encourages us to exercise our will and choose something higher, something nobler, something altogether more beautiful. Paul urges us to do exactly that. "...fill your minds," he says, "with those things that are good and that deserve praise: things that are true, noble, right, pure, lovely, and honourable." [Phil.4:8] We could make a good start by counting our blessings; the number will far exceed what we presently imagine. And we should remember and give some serious thought to answered prayer, and to the overabundant generosity of the God who has answered. If we were to do only these two things, reflectively and prayerfully, we would soon begin to see that the imagined and improper reality of what might be, or of what might have been, is eclipsed by the godly fullness of what is, of what we are and of what we have.

We could do another thing too: we could ask the Lord to dream his dreams in us, to breathe his creative life into our imaginations, and to allow us the pleasure and the honour of seeing his purposes come into being in what we are, what we do and what we create. Let's ask the Lord to share even a little of his creative imagination with us and then give us the courage to partner with him in bringing his dreams to birth. Perhaps, taking a lesson from our grand-daughters, we could include in our morning prayers one that goes something like, "What are we going to make together today, Lord?"

NEW YEAR'S RESOLUTIONS

I will bring joy, wrapped up with fancy ribbons;
And I will laugh with the exuberance of gibbons.

I will offer champagne, and not stale ale;
I will send cheques in the post, and not junk mail.

I will be a willow tree, and not a wall;
I will be the spring, and not the fall.

I will paint in colour, and not in black and white;
I will be the height of noon, and not the dead of night.

I will be a can, and not a can't;
I will be a shall, and not a shan't.

I will be a winning smile, and not a gloomy frown;
I will be the rising sun, and not its going down.

I will be a china shop, and not a raging bull;
Not a glass half empty, but a glass half full.

I will be a listening ear, and not a blabbing mouth;
Not a cold north-easterly, but a warm wind from the south.

I will put my neighbour first, and not well down the list;
I will stand with open palms, and not with tightened fists.

I will treat each moment as one I shouldn't miss;
Each day, not as a burden, but as a treasured gift.

Psalm 51 is said to have been composed by David after his adultery with Bathsheba. Here, as a prayer, is a shortened version of that psalm, which we can read in the full knowledge that our sins have all been covered by Jesus in his death on the cross.

A PRAYER

Lord, be merciful to me,
Because your love knows no bounds.
I have done wrong, and I admit it.
I have been sinful from the day I was born,
And you are right to judge me.
But you do not ask for burnt offerings;
The sacrifice that you require
Is a humble and repentant heart.
Cleanse me from sin, Lord;
Wash me, and I shall be whiter than snow.
Create a pure heart in me,
And put a new and loyal spirit in me.
Help me to be obedient,
And let me rejoice again
In the wonder of your salvation.

13

Burying Loot

Joshua 7

I WONDER IF YOU HAVE EVER COME ACROSS ANYTHING buried. You probably have, but I bet I'm one of the few to have found half the contents of a bathroom. Some years ago, while digging a pond at the bottom of our garden, I found pieces of sink, chunks of bath, and a hundred and one tiles, and while I was unearthing all this stuff, I was quietly thanking the previous owner of our house for all this extra work he had given me. He must have thought, *I'll chuck it all in here. It will save me umpteen trips to the tip, and nobody will ever find it.* Wrong! But I have a nice pond there now, and I also unearthed a few interesting things like old bottles with dates and brand imprints. In fact, it became a bit of a game, guessing what we might find next.

We all love to find things. You only have to watch *Time Team* to see the thrill of unearthing something long buried. And look at all those documentaries about Tutankhamen and grave robbers, and films like *The Mummy, Indiana Jones* and *Tomb Raider.* We can't get enough. Personally, I prefer the more subtle stuff, like that bit in *Amélie* where she roots about under the wall and pulls out a tin of childhood treasures. Isn't it good when that happens? We're sorting out the loft and we come across something we haven't seen for years, a box of valueless objects that were once, and still are, worth a fortune to us.

In Joshua 7 we have a famous burial of treasure. The context is the victory over Jericho. Just before the collapse of the walls, Joshua makes it very plain that apart from Rahab and her family, "the city and everything in it must be totally destroyed as an offering to the Lord" and that "everything made of silver, gold, bronze, or iron is set apart for the Lord". [Josh.6:17-19] It is made very clear too that if these instructions are not carried out, the people will bring destruction on themselves. At this point, the priests blow their trumpets, the men shout and those huge walls fall down as promised. You would think that after seeing a miracle like that, you would do as you were told. Well, almost everybody does.

But Achan finds a beautiful Babylonian cloak, some silver and some gold, and he likes them so much that he keeps them for himself and buries them under his tent. If this were a pantomime, we would all be shouting, "No, Achan, don't touch that stuff! It will bring you nothing but grief." But it isn't a pantomime, and Achan is there alone and probably thinking, "I shouldn't really be doing this, but these are such lovely things, and I've never had anything like them. All those years in the desert, and what have I got to show for it? Don't I deserve a little something? And they are so small compared with the tons of stuff that we've found. Nobody will miss them, and how will anybody know?"

Temptations have worked like this ever since the first one in Genesis 3. We know what God has said, but the more we think about it, the more it doesn't seem right. "He can't have meant it that way, surely? It doesn't seem fair. And why can't I have a say in all this? Why is God always trying to put me down? Why is he always treating me as if I don't matter? I have rights too, don't I? I'll go along with most things, but surely even God won't begrudge me some independence? Independence is a good thing, after all." Whenever I have sinned knowingly, I think that a lot of those thoughts have been going through my head. We justify ourselves. We make it right. We make God wrong. We set ourselves up in his place. Then we do it.

Achan's treasures are of two sorts: those to be destroyed and those to be dedicated to God. Either way, they aren't his to keep. God would have had his reasons for making these rules. Certainly it was a reminder that it was God and not the Israelites who had flattened Jericho. He was allowing them no personal trophies. For all of us there is that moment when we come to God and ask forgiveness for all that's past. Always God pardons us, lifts us up and sends us on our way. And that's all right to begin with, and maybe for ever. But many of us know that we have kept a few trophies, a sin or two that aren't all that serious (are they?) and which won't make any difference to anything (will they?). We like them; we run to them in the darkness. We know it's not quite right, but they provide some comfort. It isn't any good Achan excusing himself by saying that there were a thousand things he didn't take. He took only three, but that was still three too many. You may be obedient in every respect but one, but that's still one too many.

Achan hides his treasure. It's almost certain that nobody else will be aware of your hidden sin or disobedience, but don't kid yourself that it's hidden from God. And don't believe that it will always stay hidden. God may not choose to bring it to everyone's view, but, as contradictory as this may seem, you should hope that he will bring it into some sort of light so that at least you will see it for what it is. Your hidden sin or disobedience will disable your spiritual growth; for your own good it needs to be got rid of. A Christian cannot expect to have a vibrant and dynamic spiritual life while such a thing is tolerated. It must be brought up from the darkness and confessed. Fortunately for us, our God is able and willing to forgive us, and a fresh start is always there to be made. Don't take it lightly though. The little things we have clung to may be the most difficult to hand over.

And this is serious, for while we are disobedient or harbour secret sins, we limit the powerful and ongoing movement of God and we may become a hindrance to his Spirit and his work. We may think, like Achan does, that our disobedience will have no effect on anything at all. We may just concede that it is affecting us in some way – perhaps in some way that we can't quite put our finger on – but surely it's absurd to think that our personal sin could have repercussions on the lives of others? We imagine that these trifles will have no effect on the great scheme of things, but when the Israelites move to their next battle they are hopelessly defeated, and God grants them no success until this disobedience has been unmasked and dealt with. Later, after Achan's death, they have no such trouble in battle and they move on confidently and successfully.

Notice too that Achan's disobedience occurred after a great victory for the Israelites. You might think that the miraculous crushing of Jericho would be sufficient to impress the need for obedience upon all those present. What else have they done since arriving in front of the city but do exactly what God has told them to do? And look at the results. But that's not always the way it works. So often it's not when things are tough that we are disobedient but when everything is rosy. It makes sense: when you are up against it, you will do anything to keep God on your side, but when the sun's shining on you, that's a different matter. You're doing fine. Life's a breeze. God is not quite as necessary as he was. You've got a bit of leeway. We are back to Adam and Eve again; we want a bit of leeway when we have been given freedom. What a pity it is that we sometimes prefer the thrill of a moment to the glory of eternity.

ALL OTHER RUBBISH

In unattractive plastic, blue and bold,
Three swing bins stand
In the side-chapel
Where coffee is served,
And on them signs in black and gold.
To the left "Recyclables"
Like cups, the right hand receptacle
For "Grounds and Leaves";
And there in the middle,
Containing very little,
"All Other Rubbish".

Three crosses also stand
In the side-chapel
Where grace and mercy are served.
These too bear signs,
Nailed to the wood
Like prayer requests
By those who have stopped and looked
And stopped again.
To the left "Hope", to the right "Despair";
And there in the middle,
On a cross filled to overflowing
As if with filthy rags
And torn-off strips from plastic bags,
"All Other Rubbish".

A PRAYER

Lord,
I have acted as if light were darkness
And darkness light,
But I have not come close to fooling you;
And I have claimed that I have given
Everything to you,
But you have seen through me so easily.
Why would I ever think
That I could hide the smallest thing from you?

Lord,
Help me to understand that when I keep
My one small thing from you,
I keep from you my everything.
Help me to understand that when I offer up
This one small thing to you,
I offer up my everything,
Just as you offer your everything to me,
Not holding back,
Not keeping even one small thing
Just for yourself.

14

Unearthing Loot

1 John 1:1-10

ONE OF THE THINGS WORTH NOTING ABOUT DISOBEDI-
ence, and perhaps particularly about repeated disobedience, is that the
promise is everything, the anticipation is all. It doesn't seem to matter
that so many of our previous anticipated moments have proved in the
event disappointing, unfulfilling or empty, because the next time will
be different. This next time will be that one time when we shall be
satisfied, taken out of ourselves, made complete. Except, of course, that
the reverse is true. With each bite the meal becomes less satisfying, we
find ourselves emptier, and our lack of satisfaction and of fulfilment
deepens. On each occasion, the sweet carrot becomes a mightier stick
to beat us.

Contrast this with our experience of God, whom we often do not
anticipate as keenly as we anticipate our disobedience. I would love to
say that without fail I have always looked forward with overwhelming
joy to prayer, to worship and to being in the presence of God with the
people of God, but the truth is that I haven't always anticipated this
encounter very keenly. At times I have been casual about it, bored by it
or even resentful. But after the event, more often than not the opposite
is true. When I have allowed myself to be caught up in the Lord, I find,
to my surprise, that I am satisfied and fulfilled, and often my sense of
completeness is in direct proportion to my earlier feelings; the worse I
felt then, the better I am now.

Psalm 34 encourages us to taste and see that the Lord is good. Our
anticipation of God is not necessarily sweet before the experience
happens; our anticipation of disobedience is always sweet before it
happens. Our experience of God is sweet as we taste or, very often, as
we look back: "The Lord has helped us all the way." [1.Sam.7:12] Our
experience of disobedience is never sweet as we look back: "As soon as
they had eaten it, they were given understanding and realised that they
were naked." [Gen.3:7] Thus it is that the people of God look back and
remember, and then they move on with a firm road beneath their feet.

In disobedience we move into a future we resolutely insist will be firm, even though our every experience of such things in the past has been of shifting sand. "This time it will be different," we tell ourselves, if we tell ourselves anything at all. But it won't, because it can't be, though we will tell ourselves the same thing again next time. And here lies the temptation: not the thing itself, which is simply disobedience, but the voice which persuades us that all will be well. "Did God really say...?"

The results on the individual will be quite different too. We may fear an encounter with God, but God is loving as well as being holy and just, and if we let him, he will rebuild us. He will begin to put the fragmented parts back together. Disobedience works in the opposite fashion. It fragments; it divides and rules. Our disobedience may not have a physical effect – though it sometimes does – but it most certainly will have an emotional and a spiritual effect. Like St Paul we find ourselves doing what we don't want to do. [Rom.7:19] If our disobedience is habitual, we increasingly lack the will to do what we do want to do. We begin to hate ourselves for our weaknesses; we hear two voices and we despair. Divided within ourselves, trying to serve two masters, we become spiritually ineffective. In Tolkien's *Lord of the Rings*, although Gollum's precious ring has brought nothing but pain, misery and death, still it is so beautiful that he must have it, must possess it, even though he half knows that it will end up possessing him, that it is already possessing him.

"They were very beautiful," says Achan. The object of our dis-obedience will always seem beautiful; it will always be the one thing we need to make all the other things right. But we seldom stop to make the necessary comparison: beautiful compared with what? Adam and Eve just had to have that one extra thing, that one beautiful, desirable thing, and they ignored the fact that in that perfect place, a place shared with their perfect God, it was the only thing they didn't have – in the whole world! It's the same with Achan's treasure, the desirability of which we must see in comparison to the very real treasure of, among other things, freedom from slavery, the fatherhood of the one true God, physical protection and the promise of prosperity – all of which may not seem at first sight particularly beautiful, but this is because we're not looking at them properly; we're taking them for granted.

The fact is that in comparison to what we are taking for granted, our 'beautiful treasure' is simply an illusion. We think we are in the presence of a table-groaning banquet, but in reality the table is bare. We stay glued to this insignificant 'beautiful' thing because we resist the truly beautiful, and when the truly beautiful comes to us in a thousand different ways we do our best to avoid it or we pretend it isn't there. Or we say it's simply too big for us, which in truth it is, but in Jesus, God rearranges things so that it isn't.

Fortunately for us, even though we may share Achan's guilt, we do not have to share his fate. "But if we confess our sins to God, he will keep his promise and do what is right: he will forgive us our sins and purify us from all our wrongdoing." [1 Jn.1:9] Really though, it's not simply a case of confessing with our lips, because if we're serious about this, it will mean digging up the treasure and handing it over to the Lord. So, in case you think that what I'm recommending is just too difficult, perhaps I can encourage you with a personal encounter of my own. Not that long ago I decided it was time to do a little spiritual spring cleaning, and as I did so the Lord gave me what I think is the most beautiful picture I have so far received from him. In the picture I was kneeling at the altar of our church, and in my outstretched hands I was offering to the Lord some of the rubbish I needed to hand over. It really did look like the sort of rubbish you would put in your bin, and I was asking myself why on earth the Lord would want this stuff and what he could possibly do with it. Then Jesus was there, standing next to me, and as he lifted the rubbish from me it turned into jewellery in his hands, with bright gemstones of every colour. Moving forward to lay these things on the altar, he picked out one particularly large stone and held it up, admiring it in the sunlight and clearly delighted by it. Then he looked at me and smiled. "I think we'll keep this one," he said, "and we'll put it in our Father's crown."

I couldn't have imagined that if I'd tried, but it was a picture which reminded me immediately of some words I had seen only a few days before on the cover of an edition of the Church Mission Society's *Prayerlines*, relating to earthquakes in Nepal. The words had made a big impression on me and they had been bouncing around in my head. Now here they were again, in a context I had not at all expected: "Jesus makes beautiful things out of dust."

AND THERE IT IS AGAIN

Sometimes,
On a bad day,
I think
I'll throw it all away,
Pack it in,
Chuck it out,
Trash it,
Bin it,
Because
There's nothing
Whatsoever
In it.
And it doesn't seem to matter
What the cause is.
Something shatters
My equilibrium, forces
(Or so it seems)
My well-deserved response:
An argument perhaps,
A death
Or disappointment,
Unwelcome news,
A friend whose
Comments have offended,
A relationship that's ended.
Maybe I haven't got my way
Or had my say;
No-one's treated me
As number one today.
Whatever.
A child would stamp his feet
And cry;
I simply tap my feet
And wonder why
I've set sail
Upon this ship of fools
That's going nowhere.

Then,
Despite my willing otherwise,
A man presents himself for prayer,
And there it is again.
There it is again,
That presence of grace
And mercy,
A sense of gentleness
Enclosing me
And melting my heart.
Two brothers meeting
At our point of need,
The Christ in him responding
To the Christ in me.
Deep calling unto deep.

A PRAYER

Father, forgive me,
When I have lived a double life;
When I have tried to serve two masters;
When I have given ear so readily
To that sweet voice of temptation
And gone my own way so thoughtlessly.
There is no God but you; it is you
Who are my strength and my salvation.
Have mercy on me, Lord; forgive me
For following the path of my desire,
For making precious treasures out of things
That rot and crumble in my hands.
Rebuild me, Lord. Teach me your truths.
Encourage me to taste and see
That you are good, and help me give to you
The worthless idols I have collected
And so wrongly worshipped.

15

A Promise is a Promise

Genesis 15-16

WE WERE HAVING LUNCH WITH OUR YOUNGEST GRAND-
son and his parents. Mum and Dad were keen to tell us that their son
had recently learned some difficult new words, one of which was
'patience'. I could only imagine the tantrums and heartache on both
sides that had gone into the acquisition of this new vocabulary, and I
was genuinely interested to hear the little boy's definition, even though
our grandson, fully absorbed in crunching his way through some baby
kiwi fruit, appeared to have little interest in letting us hear it.
Nevertheless his dad pressed on, until there came that point where the
boy, doubtless fed up with this constant pressure to reveal his genius,
groaned, rolled his eyes, took a deep breath and said, very grudgingly,
"It means you're good at waiting." His father may or may not have got
the message.

As definitions go, it was brief and incomplete, but still, I think,
pretty good, and I won't forget it easily. Patience means being good at
waiting, which I would very much like to be but which I'm not. "Give
me patience, Lord!" I say, and the Lord gives me reasons to wait. "Not
like that, Lord!" I say. "*Just make me patient!*" But he won't, because
he can't; because it's one of those things which, despite all things being
possible for him, is simply not possible – not with an incantation and a
swish of a wand anyway.

I wish I could say that I have got everything right in my life, but I
haven't, and perhaps like everybody else there have been times when I
have said something or done something or taken a course of action that
I later regretted. Mercifully, I did not lose sight of the Lord during these
times, and he didn't for a moment give up on me. On one such occasion
I sensed these words: "Will you allow yourself to accept that what has
happened has happened, and will you allow me to turn it to good?"
My immediate reaction was that these were unnecessary questions; of
course it had happened, and why wouldn't I want it turned to good?
But nothing that comes from the Lord is unnecessary, and when I gave

some time to considering his words, I knew that I should have listened more carefully.

Allowing oneself to accept that 'what has happened has happened' is important if we're ever going to come to terms with it. Firstly, because we can be tempted to distance ourselves from the event by thinking such things as "These things don't happen to people like me, do they?" or "Surely I wasn't capable of that, was I?" or "It wasn't really my fault, was it?" Let's get it straight: yes, they do; yes, you were; and yes, it was. Secondly, because we can be tempted to dwell on the event far too much, turning it round and round in our minds, imagining how it might have been done differently, maybe trying to convince ourselves that it wasn't as bad as we remember, or perhaps believing in some sort of subconscious manner that if we think long and hard enough we might be able to change past events or even make them disappear altogether. Wrong again. And thirdly, because until we square up to what we've done, we cannot fully accept the forgiveness that comes from the Lord or from others or, importantly, from ourselves.

Please don't think that I'm suggesting that this acceptance is easy, because it isn't. Taking a good look at yourself and what you've done, and accepting that you've done it, is a very difficult thing to do. The curtains are drawn back, there are no more excuses, and it can be, if we let it be, a sinking moment. But the Lord takes no pleasure in our sinking. What he wants is the opposite, and to prove it he speaks again, with almost no pause for breath: "...and will you allow me to turn it to good?"

Will you? Allow? Allow me? Allow me to turn it to good? Why would the Lord say it like that? Why didn't he simply say, "Don't worry, it'll be all right"? Because the Lord knew that I needed more than that. Because the Lord knew that I was facing some further temptations, and the first of these was the temptation to believe that nothing good could ever come from what I had done. He was asking me if I was willing to lay down my assertions that there was a finality about it, that any way forward was impossible and that what I'd broken could never be mended. He was giving me a choice. If I chose, I could persist in my belief that all the pieces would remain lying randomly all over the floor, or I could hand the broken pieces to him and let him, *allow him*, in ways that I could not possibly imagine, to put them back together and create a thing of beauty. Not my will, but yours. Not my way, but yours.

A second temptation addressed by the Lord in his question to me was the temptation to try to turn it to good myself, in other words to fix it. The Lord comes to Abraham and tells him that he will have a son and that through Abraham and his son and the succeeding generations all the earth will be blessed. What happens next? Nothing. For year after year, nothing. And as nothing comes from nothing, let's sort it out ourselves. "The Lord said he'd give us a son, but the clock's ticking and it isn't really possible anyway, so what's the harm in making it happen our way? Maybe that's what the Lord meant after all?" The rest, as they say, is history. And what a history. That's the way it is with us: the Lord gives us a promise, but very annoyingly for us he rarely goes into any detail, and over time the promise can become a little blurred in our ears. It's then that it seems perfectly reasonable to think that we should fix it ourselves. But the Lord asks, "Will you allow *me*...?" And we really should. Let's face it, he'll do it much better than we will; we would only add insult to injury and break the fragments into ever smaller pieces.

I was prompted to write this because it wasn't only one word that our grandson had learned but two. The first, as you know, was 'patience'. Somewhat improbably, the second was 'trust'. Our grandson had no intention of defining this word as well, so I'll do it myself: trust is believing that somebody is completely reliable and then relying on them; it's believing that they are who they say they are and that they will do what they have said they will do. It is what we already know of the Lord: I am who I say I am, and I will do what I have promised to do. Trust and patience are closer than brothers. If I trust, I will be patient, and in my patience is my trust. So, in saying to me what he did, the Lord was coming to me as he did to Abraham, with an acceptance of me as I am, with his offer of friendship, with a promise of blessing and with a gentle challenge to trust and be patient.

And there's hardly a day goes by when I don't come to the Lord, reminding him of his offer and saying, "Yes, I will allow you to turn it to good. Please give me the grace to let you." And when that's too difficult, I go back to Abraham and Sarah. And when that's too hard, the Lord arranges for me to have lunch with my grandson, so that before he beats me black and blue with his newest light sabre, the little boy can remind me of my heavenly Father's promises. Because my patience and my trust are not yet what they could be.

IN THE WATER'S EDGE

Jesus came down to the shore;
Saw early morning light
Bouncing off the calm sea
Like the cries of fishermen;
Bathed his hands and his feet
In the water's edge;
Felt again its life and its freshness,
Becoming himself stillness,
And knowing,
As no other person knew or would know,
That this sea,
These hills,
This water's edge,
These fishermen, shouting with disbelief
And leaping from their boats,
Their existence,
His existence even,
Flowed like an unstoppable river
From that moment,
That one quiet moment of submission
On another hill,
A moment
That these fishermen,
Crashing like excited children
Through the splashing shallows,
Had simply slept away.

A Prayer

Heavenly Father,
My collection of regrets resemble souvenirs;
There's something new from almost every trip:
Words said, words left unsaid;
Deeds done and not done; a look
That brought someone a little lower;
Encouragements that seldom reached my lips;
A risk I never took, a risk I took which failed;
Acts of hospitality which lived
No longer than an afterthought. And all,
In summary: If only...

Heavenly Father,
May I bring each one of these to you,
And as I do, will you receive them,
Unattractive as they are,
And lift them from me, change them
Into something beautiful and good
That blesses now,
And blesses even in times past,
Each child of God I have,
With words or deeds, unblessed?

16

Caring for Plants

Jonah 3-4

MY WIFE SOMETIMES BUYS HERSELF A BUNCH OF FLOWERS. I know that it should be me buying her the flowers, but I'm not very good at that, so she buys them for herself. Maybe she pretends it was me who bought them, but I doubt it. She probably looks at the flowers and thinks what a mean so-and-so I am. Needless to say, that's what I think when I look at them, and I resolve to do better. As I usually fail in this, you'll understand why the sight of flowers in our house always makes me feel guilty. That is, until some chrysanthemums sprang a surprise attack.

We'd had them for a fortnight, and they were ready to join similar bouquets in the compost, when one Saturday morning we noticed that the flowers had taken on a grey, furry look, as if a bag of dust had been emptied over them. On closer inspection we saw thousands of tiny insects, like blackfly, the product of the night's hideous hatching. They were crawling up the walls and across the carpet, and they left a black stain, like ink, when squashed. Soon we were scratching at various parts of our body, but there was worse: they might already have found the orchid.

Now, I'm not really a plant person; plants don't do much, they just sit there. They may flower from time to time, but they are so fearfully slow at it. I love them when television speeds them up, brambles growing at fifty miles an hour, for example, but I can't get excited about them. Except, that is, for our orchid, a gift from our youngest daughter on Mother's Day. It came with a huge spike of beautiful pink blooms which seemed to last for ever. And then, when for ever was finally over, it did what orchids do: it sank into a period of depression, a dull, leafy green gloom, and we settled down to waiting...

...For about eighteen months. Weird, pointy things came groping for air, but they were roots, interesting only when they attached themselves to the wallpaper when we weren't looking. But there was no sign of flowers, and this wasn't fair, as this orchid was well looked after. My wife sprayed it with soothing mist and fed it. She spoke to it and asked it simply to be itself, something few of us are. And when I'd reached that point of near insanity where I found myself harbouring jealousy towards a plant, it happened. Something different began to appear, and we could not believe our good fortune.

So you can see why we hovered – and hoovered – around our orchid for the rest of the day. We put our eyes to every surface, looking for one more insect on its way to destroy it, and then at last we breathed a sigh of relief; we were safe. Until, that is, home group met the next day, and we found ourselves talking about our orchid, displayed with pride on a shelf centre stage. Our friend Bill got up to examine our prize, but Bill is unsteady on his pins and, losing his balance, reached out to the shelf for support. You need to know that it was me who put up the shelf, and I'm no handyman. Carol, knowing this, ran to Bill's rescue, but I was the only person who knew that she had rushed to save the plant, not Bill, and she stood there, to all appearances very casually, but all the while exerting the same upward pressure on the shelf as Bill was exerting downwards.

I'm not the only person to have given such importance to a plant. The prophet Jonah was also fond of a plant, though most people remember him only for the big fish. I guess that's not surprising; people very rarely appear to spend three days alive inside a fish, whereas slugs eat plants all the time. However, whilst the fish is important here, the plant is more important.

Imagine for a moment that you're Jonah, and God tells you to go to the capital city of an enemy country and preach a message of judgement. Naturally, and just like Jonah, you won't want to do that so, also like Jonah, you'll hop on a boat bound for Spain. The problem, together with your feelings of guilt, won't seem as big from the balcony of your apartment in Benidorm, not that you actually get there. But we've run ahead. First we have to decide why we've run off to Spain. Some reasons might be: the Assyrians are my enemy; I don't like them; there are hundreds and thousands of them, and that's just in Nineveh; they are violent people; they won't listen to me; they will laugh at me and probably beat me up; they may even kill me.

That's what you might think. In fact Jonah's reason for not wishing to go to Nineveh is nowhere near as predictable, and if we're not careful we can miss it, even though it's as plain as day. Certainly, he doesn't like the Assyrians, and perhaps there is an element of fear too, but the thing which really puts him off going to preach the message of God is that he knows that if those horrible people repent, God will forgive them.

As we know, they do repent and God does forgive them, and Jonah is hopping mad. "I knew you'd do that!" he exclaims. "I just knew it!" These Assyrians were foreigners, enemies, wicked, *and they didn't deserve God's forgiveness.* Having discovered inside the fish that he was incapable of outwitting his God, Jonah still thinks he knows better. He understands how his God works, he knows about God's patience, kindness and readiness to forgive, but in the case of the Assyrians he thinks these things are out of place and if that is the way God is going to play the game then he might as well die. So, like a spoiled child, he stamps his feet a few times.

Enter the plant. It grows quickly, and Jonah becomes attached to it, not only because it's attractive but also because it shades him from the sun, and the sun is a scorcher in Assyria. Jonah can settle in and live in the shade of that plant for any amount of time, except that God has decided that this amount of time is going to be rather short. Needless to say, Jonah is hopping mad again. "What are you playing at?" rails Jonah. "I really liked that plant." "Precisely," says God.

Do I care for my orchid more than I care for someone I don't like? This is such an important question that God won't let me escape it. "Love your enemies," Jesus says, "and pray for those who persecute you, so that you might become the children of your Father in heaven." [Matt.5:44,45] It isn't good enough to know that God is like that; God insists that *we* should be like that too. It's hard, and it doesn't come naturally, but it's what God wants. Fortunately for us, God gives us some help. As my son has some of my characteristics, and as I share some of my earthly father's, so too I share in my heavenly Father's nature as I open myself to the work of his Spirit. There is, then, an enabling, but there are times too when it takes an effort of the will. "Do it," says God. "Just do it." There isn't any other way. The alternative is to catch a boat to Spain on a windy day, which I have done, and there really isn't much fun to be had.

Think of somebody who in your opinion doesn't deserve God's love and forgiveness as much as you do. Allow God to show you that however unfair it may seem, he loves this person as much as he loves you. Now be a child of your Father in heaven and pray for this person. No grumbles. Just do it. And when you're next tending to your favourite plant, spare a godly thought for the person who lives next door. Better still, go and visit them. Take them a bunch of flowers.

One of my favourite photographs is of our eldest grandson, then aged two, waiting at a bus stop. Around him are several other people, not one of whom he knows, sitting, standing or simply walking past. Our grandson is side on, and his face is hidden by the hood of his coat pulled up over his head. There is, therefore, no expression to see, and I often look at the picture and wonder what he was thinking. Maybe, at least in my imagination, something like this...

THE NEXT BUS

The sun's going down at the edge of the town,
Turning yellows and reds into shadowy brown,
And I think that I'd rather be anywhere else
But here, on this seat, with this random collection
Of travellers sharing no interconnection,
And hearing the noise of musicians on corners
Who wail to the air like professional mourners,
The wind sticking knives in the unfeeling street,
Blowing wrappers from sweets into piles by my feet;
And the shoppers pass by, and the school children shout,
Some youths in the alley are messing about,
A child in a pushchair is sucking his thumb,
And a man in a suit is spitting out gum,
Oh, when will the next bus come?

Oh, when will the next bus come?
And where will the next bus go,
On its roundabout route that's so painfully slow,
Going here, going there, going every old where,
'cause the way that they take is never direct
And we should have the means, I believe, to select
From a list, "Go straight there!"
But they don't, they don't care,
They just drive here and there
In a haphazard line that eats up my time,
And they take me to areas I don't want to be
Seeing people in places I don't want to see:
The rich and the poor, and the plain in between,
The avenues where everyone lives like the Queen,
And just round the corner the people in boxes
And foxes in bins, and then it begins

Like the birth of a fungus, that fear
That creeps in, shrieking, "Don't drop me here!"

When and where, where and when, then the question will be:
"Who's going to be on the next bus with me?"
My parents, my sister, my comfort zone friends
I'll accept, they're all safe, but that's where it ends.
But as for the others, though it's not now correct,
Between you and me I'd be glad to eject:
The cougher, the sniffer, the girl who just sneezes,
The large man who squeezes my personal space;
The kid drinking milk and the one eating cheeses,
The boy with the mobile glued on to his face;
That impolite man who's refusing to stand –
The one in the cap – who won't lend a hand
To the woman with child who's now stuck in the aisle
And sways with exhaustion for mile after mile;
The lady who smells and the man who keeps scratching,
The old couple behind in wool hats that are matching;
It may not be right; I don't want to condemn,
But why must I be on the same bus as them?

So, round in a circle and back to the top,
Meaning: "Where is the next bus going to stop?"
Will it be in a place that I've been to before,
With familiar smells and the toys on the floor,
The narrow-street noises, the passing of trains,
The neighbourhood cat that leaves gifts by the door,
The arrival of planes, the insistence of rain,
The creak of that floorboard again and again?
Or now somewhere different, unthought-of, unknown,
A place that I'd never consider as home,
Where the strangeness of everything fits like a skin,
Where the mouth wants a sentence it cannot begin,
Where the air is like brass and the grass cuts your feet,
And you seek some reflection in faces you meet
To dispel that cold dread that seeps through your bones
That among all these people you're completely alone...
But then rings the hope, in my heart, like a bell,
That my friend, who goes with me, will get off there as well!

A PRAYER

Father God,
You choose to send me on a mission;
I choose to take a holiday.
You entrust me with your message of salvation;
I put it in my personal belongings.
You show me to an empty seat
Near people I don't like;
I say, "Please put me on the next plane out."

Father God, forgive me,
For having worshipped with my lips
But not with my obedience;
For applauding all your fine commands,
But then ignoring them;
For being in wonder at your hands and feet
But refusing to let them live and move in me.

Father God,
I was wrong to take the long detour.
Help me back on to the right path;
Walk with me, lead me and let me find
Such pleasure in allowing myself, at last,
To do what you have asked.

17

The Credit Crunch

Matthew 18:1-5; 20:20-28

CAROL AND I WERE ON PRAYER MINISTRY AFTER THE morning service, when Sarah came up looking stressed. Having for some years enjoyed a very rewarding job, she had recently been made redundant and was looking to the Lord for help. I was a bit hesitant at first, but then I took the bull by the horns and prayed with what I believed was some degree of confidence. I thought that I had taken a few risks in my praying, gone out on a limb, been a little like the pestering widow in the parable. But Jesus had encouraged us to do just that, so why not? During the following week I continued to pray for Sarah and for her new job. "Surprise her, Lord," I said. "Do something amazing."

A fortnight later, at a charity event, we were sitting at a table with several others when Sarah came across, and addressing our companions rather than us, or so it seemed to me, she said that during the week she had been offered a job and could start immediately. All of which was wonderful news, so why, sitting underneath this conversation, was I not rejoicing?

Partly, I think, because there is nothing like encouragement. We pray regularly as part of a prayer ministry team, sometimes hesitantly, often feeling that our faith is completely insufficient for the task, and only occasionally do we hear whether or not God has answered our prayers. More and more I suspect that he has, but it is so helpful to know that he has, because the next time I pray, I will pray with greater faith, confident in the fact that the last time we prayed, God answered, and he answered abundantly.

But that's only half the truth. No, if I'm honest it's much less than half the truth, because I know that a lot of what was going on here was to do with who was taking the credit. I had thought that some sort of maturing had been going on in me, because I felt increasingly, and honestly, happy that God should receive all the thanks and all the praise. And perhaps some maturing had happened, but this experience

103

stopped me in my tracks and made me wonder whether I'd come as far as I thought I had. After all, if I serve others for the sake of Jesus and the gospel, then whatever credit I may or may not receive in the present life, I will one day hear, "Well done, you good and faithful servant!" [Matt.25:23] And that should be enough.

I wish it were, but all too often it's my experience that temptations to pride rear their ugly heads in the holiest of places. Sometime before the incident narrated above, we had prayed for healing with a man suffering from a bad back. I'm glad to say that the problem disappeared. Then more recently a woman suffering from similar symptoms, and who had heard about this previous answer to prayer, approached us for prayer for herself. Two things then happened. One, I was thrilled to be asked; for me, praying for others is a joy and a privilege. Two, I felt rather pleased with myself, and I wondered if for me this might not be the beginning of a significant ministry to bad backs! How ridiculous is that? Carol doesn't suffer from these absurd delusions, but I have to be constantly on my guard.

"Look at me!" is what I'm wanting to say, and it makes me feel a little better to know that I'm not the only one who wants to say it. In Luke 9:46-48 an argument breaks out among Jesus' disciples as to how they rank in order of importance. You might think, as I probably did, that this occurs immediately after Jesus calls them. That would make sense. After all, is a fisherman better than a tax-collector? Is the first to be called more important than the twelfth? If we're brothers, is my older brother higher up in the pecking order than I am? But in Luke's narrative this argument follows, not precedes, their being sent out by Jesus to minister to others. It comes *after* "the disciples left and travelled through all the villages, preaching the Good News and healing people everywhere". In other words – and this surprised me – they were now some way along the road, and still they wanted to take the credit, each man more than the next if he could.

Jesus treats them patiently. After all, he knows what's going on. In Jesus' post-baptism temptations Satan suggests that Jesus should throw himself from the highest point of the Temple. [Lk.4:1-13] The devil reminds Jesus that according to Scripture, God's angels will come and save him and, we might suppose, the world will treat him as a superhero. So now Jesus takes a child and shows his disciples what one of God's superheroes looks like: not big, not strong, not a great achiever, not way out ahead of the rest. He is lowly and apparently unimportant. He has no claim to credit.

104

Then Jesus takes the idea a step further. "If you welcome a child in my name," he says, "you welcome me." This isn't what we might expect either. He doesn't say, "If you restore sight to a blind man, you welcome me," which is maybe what we were thinking he should say. For Jesus there is no place for our all too frequent, self-indulgent, spiritual one-upmanship, that almost instinctive tariff of difficulty that we create in our heads: three healings are worth one deliverance, but a resurrection from the dead is equal to all four put together. Greatness, he says, lies not in achieving but in serving, and it very often lies in serving the sort of people we would prefer not to serve and in the sort of places we would prefer not to serve them. When Jesus says, "Heal the sick," I'm happy to be involved. When he says, "Go and visit prisoners in their prisons," or, even worse, "Be generous and hospitable," I look the other way and assume he must be talking to somebody else.

And it doesn't stop there, because the sort of servanthood Jesus is talking about isn't a one-evening-a-week shift at a fancy restaurant, where you receive a good wage, a free three-course meal and a pocketful of tips from wealthy customers. Paul and others in the New Testament are making a good point when they call themselves "slaves of Jesus Christ". They are saying that they have become something that the world has great difficulty in understanding: voluntary slaves, offering themselves in the service of God and of others. But – here's the thing – it's a beautiful slavery because, contrary to expectation, it's a slavery that releases us. We no longer have to weigh up the value of this bit of service against that bit of service before doing it, and nor do we have to worry about the success of it afterwards. And certainly we have no need – we have no right – to trouble ourselves about who is going to take the credit.

It will take time, practice and a lot of grace. It may take a deliberate shift in our choice of words, spoken or unspoken, as was brought home to me very gently by a minister from whom I had received some helpful prayer and counselling. A week or so after the latter had taken place, I thanked him again. "God is good," he replied. "Yes," I agreed. "He is good, but you had a part in it too." He smiled. "God is *very* good," he said.

AT THE ALTAR RAIL

Differences in height diminish at the altar rail.
See, for instance, how they come together, this family,
From the careless separation of disjointed days
And squeeze one against the other, voluntarily,
As if those casual moments in the snaking line
Had brought about the full maturing of their lives.

Notice how the eldest son, thick-necked, shoulders wide-beamed,
Broader than father or mother, bows his head, whispers
Amen, makes an offering of strength and voice, it seems;
Young man, ready to hold the world, his younger sister
Ready to be held, soft at the edges, her eyes fierce-
-ly gentle, heart preparing for the sword that comes to pierce.

Look at the twin boys, just now jostling with each other
In the queue; how their fists, fresh from fighting, unforced open,
Empty-handed to receive the bread and wine, their mother
Grateful for this promise of peace, this pause so often
Longed for, her husband pressed close, eyes steady on the cross,
Asking that not one of these, his little ones, be lost.

A PRAYER

Heavenly Father,
I come to you, like Naaman,
Desperate for healing, and ready
To do anything; anything, of course,
Except that thing you ask, to lower
Myself into an unimportant stream, and wash.
Forgive me, Father, for having protested
So loudly. Forgive me, even in my healing,
For coveting your glory.
Help me, instead, to seek no credit
For myself, and to walk the humble path
Which Jesus walked: Jesus, Saviour,
Servant of servants.

18

God of Small Things

Luke 16:1-13

IF YOU WANT A LITTLE TEST FOR YOURSELF, I SUGGEST YOU volunteer for the church coffee rota. I wish I could say that Carol and I had volunteered to join ours, but several years ago when we were asked to join, we felt we probably should, so we did. On our very first coffee duty I regretted this, because while doing our preparations before the service, I very quickly fell into two big holes.

The first of these falls came about when I discovered that the third helper hadn't turned up, leaving us two newbies to do everything ourselves, including nipping out to get some milk. Of course, I had no way at that moment of knowing the cause of our colleague's absence. It's perfectly possible that he was seriously ill or had suffered a sudden bereavement. He might, even as I stood carefully measuring coffee powder, have been shooing a herd of cows from his vegetable patch, or he might, even on his way to church, have crossed over the road to help a poor man who had been beaten up and robbed. Maybe right then, as I stood muttering to myself, he was in a hospital sitting by the same man's bedside. Who knew? I certainly didn't, but that didn't prevent me from feeling pretty cheesed off.

I'm glad to say that after some years of serving coffee I have discovered that the absence of colleagues is exceptionally rare and that even when it does happen, I am now less affected by it. However, on that very first occasion I will admit to having spent the service which followed in a state of advanced peevishness, a condition not helped by the smell of percolated Colombian that hung on me like a shroud. I wasn't thinking, "How great is our God!" Instead I was wondering why our not very great colleague hadn't brought the milk *as he was supposed to do.* I wasn't pondering the pleasures of gathering with all the saints around the crystal sea. I was asking myself if, after all, it would be much more pleasurable *not* to gather with them, or, indeed, if any one of them apart from me would think it important to arrive at the crystal sea on time. *With the milk!* In other words, I'd judged him out of heaven, which maybe seemed all right at the time, because doubtless I believed I was still in heaven, but it doesn't seem all right now.

Judging others is something that Jesus forbids, but we do it anyway, perhaps because it seems such a very small thing. Children do it from very young. By middle age we're experts at it and do it for a pastime, forgetting, if we ever knew, that in our judging we've taken on a role that God has reserved for himself. It's his place to judge, not mine, and if I take it from him it will have an effect on me that I wouldn't really want if I thought much about it. I may not see it at first, and I may never see it, but my judging will make me sharper at the edges, increasingly cold and, whether I intend it or not, superior. When I judge another person, I'm really thinking, "I know better than you," and increasingly, "I *am* better than you." In my judging I belittle the other person, certainly in my mind and possibly in theirs too. It isn't such a small thing after all.

Our role, says God, is to be gracious and forgiving, to look at others through loving and not critical eyes, to build up and not tear down. Our role, to put it simply, is to treat others in the same way that God has treated us. The unforgiving servant in Jesus' parable in Matthew 18 is put in prison until the full amount owed is repaid. "That," says Jesus, "is how my Father in heaven will treat every one of you unless you forgive your brother from your heart." Reflecting later on my judgemental spirit, I sensed the Lord saying to me, "John, don't be so hard on my children. Try to remember that I paid the same high price for them as I did for you."

My other fall from grace is somewhat connected to the first, because I suspect that I started all my coffee preparations with the feeling, somewhere deep down inside me, and perhaps unexpressed even to myself, that this job was too small for me. By that I don't mean that I believed that serving coffee wasn't a worthwhile thing to do, because I knew that it was. No, this feeling was suggesting that I myself should be doing something bigger, better and more important. I would be more usefully employed, I thought, in praying with people rather than in serving them coffee. I knew that we could all do with more prayer; I doubted we were in such dire need of caffeine.

There's some truth in the latter, of course, but I'd fallen headlong into that common trap of judging one person's work against another's and ranking them in order of importance. There are those, I know, who instinctively and very beautifully choose, and appear perfectly at home with, the less glamorous forms of service. But if you're anything like me, it's the big task we want, and we think that if only God would give us a big task, a job with glory and honour attached, we'd do it better than anyone else. It would be a big task that only we could do. Well, I'm not sure we could. I think we might even make a mess of it, because we can't even do the very small task that we've already been asked to do and to which we've agreed. We easily forget Jesus' words in the parable of the talents: "You have been faithful in managing small amounts, so I will put you in charge of large amounts." [Matt.25:23] We'd prefer it to be the other way round, but he doesn't give us that luxury. So here's something I've learned the hard way. Now that I have grown to the point where I can serve coffee with a smile, I find I can participate in prayer ministry with an even bigger smile. Now that I can be relaxed on that very unusual occasion when someone doesn't turn up to serve coffee, perhaps even enjoying the extra challenge this poses, I can be more relaxed in praying with others, even when they throw in some curveball I hadn't expected.

When Jesus sets about washing the disciples' feet, Peter is taken aback by it and at first refuses. "You're the boss," he thinks, "and this has to be beneath you." But Jesus won't let Peter think like this. "If I do not wash your feet," Jesus answers, "you will no longer be my disciple." [Jn.13:8] Jesus is saying that this isn't an option; it's who he is, Servant of servants. No act of service to another is beneath him, and if Peter is to remain a disciple and a friend, he'll have to get used to it and he'll have to do the same.

And then I wondered what Jesus himself would be doing if he were present, physically, in our church on a Sunday morning. Lots of things, I guess, but I'm pretty sure that among them would be these three: he'd be serving coffee, he'd be praying with people and he'd be sitting with that guy in the corner who drifted in almost unnoticed an hour ago and who is now about to drift out again, perhaps for ever. But the man won't drift out now, because Jesus has noticed him and welcomed him. Jesus has lifted him up and given him value and identity. And whatever the man might have thought about himself when he came in, Jesus has looked him straight in the eyes and said, "You're no small thing to me."

ICING FOR JOY

Come to the head of the queue, anyone
who will clean toilets for the Lord.
Step up, take off your armour, sheathe your sword,
and minimize that grand horizon
until your pleasant vision
is, for as long as it may take, contained
in bowls of shining porcelain.
Let your heart be light. Let it dance
to the tune of cisterns flushing,
to the creak of pushing
open doors that lead you to the very heart of God.
Don't be afraid to set yourself a little lower.
Go sweep a path, devote one hour
to the childlike joy of watching dust
float carefree and content in beams of light
before you catch it. Make offerings
of small and scarcely noticed things.
Come decorate a birthday cake,
serve coffee with a smile,
walk that extra one immeasurable mile,
and God will have a smile upon his face,
and he will sing for joy
at all the works of your hands,
your tired, dirty hands,
those hands that bear the marks of grace.

A PRAYER

Father God,
How easily I take
The seat of judgement;
How readily I take on
The roles of judge and jury,
Magnifying others' faults
And misdemeanours
And belittling my own.

Father God, I would exchange
My judgement for your mercy;
I would swap my condemnation
For your forgiveness;
And I would give my blinkered view
For eyes uncluttered, light full,
Eyes that reflect your godly understanding
And your limitless compassion.

19

Healing Lessons

Acts 3:1-10

NOT LONG AFTER WE WERE MARRIED, CAROL WENT DOWN with some sort of kidney infection. We assumed that within a day or two of her taking medication it would go away, but it didn't, and after several days she was quite unwell, suffering a high temperature and beginning to hallucinate. It so happened that my brother and his fiancée had just arrived for the weekend, and something prompted me to ask if they would mind joining me in praying for my wife's healing. I wish I could remember now what we prayed and how we prayed it. All I know is that while we were praying, my wife was healed, and I don't mean that she started to feel better. I mean she was healed.

It was a moment I'll never forget. I went up to the bedroom to check on her, and there she was, sitting up, beaming from ear to ear. "A great band of warmth went through me from my head to my feet," she explained, "and I spoke in a language I didn't know." In response to our prayers, or in response to hers, or because he just wanted to do it, God had released his Spirit on her and had healed her. He had done more than that, actually. He had also given her an excitement about himself and a desire to tell others about her healing. I was as thrilled as my wife was, even though it hadn't happened to me. On the Monday morning I told a colleague at work about it. "I don't buy that," he said. "That was obviously the moment when the medicine kicked in." But he hadn't seen my wife walking and jumping, and I had.

More recently Carol went down with sciatica. It wasn't just painful, it reduced her mobility to almost zero, and she was to all intents and purposes crippled. Why was that, and why, despite much prayer from us and others, did God not heal her as he had done before? I have no idea, and I have no idea why, almost twelve months and an operation later, she found herself among the small percentage of post-operative patients suffering from recurring pain and needing a further procedure.

But I learned two things. The first is that although God may not have answered the big prayer, he did answer a lot of smaller ones. You may think that this is a cop out, and sometimes I think so myself, but this did happen. My wife's spirits remained buoyant throughout, the healthcare she received was first class, and during the many months when even a sneeze would have brought acute pain, she didn't sneeze once. In fact she remained healthy in every other respect. In my prayers one day I sensed the words, "I guard the gates." And he did.

The second lesson is much simpler, and it concerns the people who visited during those months when Carol was more or less housebound. Some did this regularly, and I bless them for it, because the effect of their visits was hugely positive. They may not have brought healing, though certainly there were those who prayed for it, but they brought other things which were, in a sense, just as important. They brought their concern, their affection, their smiles and their time. And they brought that other very precious thing, that almost indefinable something that says, "You're important to us, and we care about you." There were also many too who phoned, who texted and who sent a card, but it was the visits which had the greatest impact, not just on my wife but on me too. "Tell her we're praying for her," people would say to me, and I'd think, "Why not come and tell her yourself?"

There was an important lesson here for the two of us, and we decided that in future we would, whenever possible, try to give a face and an embrace to our concern for others. Of course, it's not always possible, but it's so easy to assume either that another person will do it or that the invalid would rather see anybody else but us. What if everybody else is thinking the same thing? What if there is no other person? What if that nagging voice inside me really is the voice of the Lord prompting me to do something that he considers right now to be the most important thing in the world? How can I not do it?

Asked about commandments, Jesus says in Matthew 22 that all the law of the Old Testament is summed up like this: "Love the Lord your God with all your heart, with all your soul, and with all your mind," and "Love your neighbour as you love yourself." He puts them in that order, and we agree that he should, but he never allows us to believe that the second of these two commandments is less significant than the first. In fact, on the evening of his arrest, when he is speaking to his friends at the last supper, he goes further: "And now I give you a new commandment: love one another. As I have loved you, so you must love one another." [Jn.13:34] Loving other people – and with the same self-giving, sacrificial love that Jesus shows to us – is Jesus' priority. And it's by showing this love, says Jesus in the next verse, that others will know we are his disciples. Just saying that we love the Lord won't do it. Standing on a soap box won't do it. Preaching the best sermon in the history of the universe won't do it. What will do it is something much easier, and of course much harder: loving your neighbour.

In Matthew 25 Jesus tells the parable of the Last Judgement in which the king, Jesus, says to the righteous, "I was hungry and you fed me, thirsty and you gave me a drink; I was a stranger and you received me in your homes, naked and you clothed me; I was sick and you took care of me, in prison and you visited me." The people look at him in amazement. "We don't remember doing that," they say. "I know you don't," says Jesus, "but when you showed kindness to someone else, you were showing kindness to me." Your act of love towards anybody is an act of love towards Jesus. We can perhaps believe this because Jesus says it, but it's still a pretty difficult thing to grasp. We'd much rather he had said the opposite, that if we love God we are already loving others, but he doesn't. He doesn't offer us that excuse, which is a real pity, because loving God, or at least thinking or saying that we love him, is often a great deal easier than loving our neighbour. And neither does he offer us that other excuse we'd really like to hear, the one that says that because I love the Lord I can treat my neighbour abominably. History would suggest that he said that too, but he didn't.

I'm going to stick my neck out here and say that if you have only half an hour to live and you can't decide between going to church and visiting somebody shut in with sciatica, then you should visit the invalid. Of course, if you have a couple of hours to live, you have sufficient time to do both.

HEALING HANDS

I couldn't take my eyes off his hands,
Anxious, I suppose, to discover in them something other,
As if I thought they'd crackle with lightning,
Be covered with gold or silver,
Sparkle like gems.
But his hands were much like my hands,
Sparkling only with the sweat of the lengthening day
And covered only with the dust of all the long way.
Truth is there was nothing in those hands
That one might consider out of the ordinary,
Except, maybe, for that gentle touch,
And except, of course, for the blind man,
Now no longer blind,
Standing shocked in the light of the sun,
Amazed at the sight of walking trees
And then of walking people
Much like himself.

So what about my hands?
Hands that have done too much
And done not nearly enough.
Hands that have shared my life with me,
Followed me, led me,
Got me into trouble and got me out of it.
Hands that once belonged to a child,
With a blob of blue paint
Here on my ring finger, and,
Spanning these thick vein ridges,
Blotches of old age that spread
Like splashes of wood stain.
What am I to make of these hands,
Hands that are much like his?
And why, when I unclench my hands,
Open them out,
And lift them to him like a gift,
Do I feel across my palms
Something like a cool breeze from the sea,

As if someone were breathing upon them,
So softly as to go almost unnoticed?

A PRAYER

Forgive me, Lord,
When I have listened intently to your words,
But have neglected to do them;
When I have worshipped you with my lips,
But have ignored you in my deeds;
When I have felt your prompt to love another,
But have loved myself instead;
When I have seen my neighbour's needs,
And looked the other way, forgetting
That when I show kindness to another,
I show kindness to my Lord.
Please help me, Lord,
To see the face of Jesus on each face I meet,
And to serve each person in the way
That I serve Him.

20

Big Brother

Luke 15:11-32

I WAS IN CHURCH THE OTHER DAY, AND WE WERE PART way into a really good song, when a little girl left her parents in a pew near me, stood in the middle of the aisle and started dancing. Now, let's stop for a moment, so that I can ask you a question: if this had happened in your church, and maybe near you, how would you have felt about it? I was fine with it, to tell you the truth. At that moment, in that place and in that song, dancing before the Lord seemed a very good thing to be doing, though I suppose I was glad it was the little girl dancing and not me. I wondered, though, how many others were happy to see her dancing, and then thoughts of the prodigal son came into my head.

It has been said that Jesus' parable of the prodigal son is the best short story ever told; it is certainly one of the most challenging. With such a title, most sermons on this parable focus on the prodigal son himself and his relationship with his father; he is the sinner returning to the arms of a gracious and forgiving God. He is, or he can be, each one of us, and maybe the story would be powerful enough if it ended at the home-coming. However, with the fatted calf sizzling away, Jesus takes us on to the scary bit.

I think we are happy to be the prodigal son. We might have wasted this and spoiled that, and we might have turned our back on God, but whatever we have or have not done, everything is now forgiven in the Father's embrace. God welcomes us back, throws a party and treats us as if nothing has happened. We can wonder whether we are good enough and ask ourselves a million questions about what will happen when we get back, but when we are at last so desperate that we are forced to put one foot in front of the other, what do we find? Our Father, running down the road to meet us. Who would not be happy about that?

The scary bit is what comes next – the big brother – and with him Jesus moves from telling us about the bad man getting it right to the good man getting it wrong. In the immediate historical context this second part would have been directed at the religious leaders of the day who appear throughout the Gospel narratives criticising and condemning Jesus for the way in which he goes about things, in this instance for the manner in which he treats outcasts and sinners, assuring them of God's generosity, love, forgiveness and the possibility of a restored relationship with their heavenly Father. Wherever Jesus goes he meets prodigals; what happens in the parable is happening everywhere in real life. The hated Zacchaeus comes down from his tree, serves tea and cakes, and makes restitution to those he has wronged. When Jesus goes home with him, Zacchaeus is coming home to the Father. The woman caught in adultery is brought out to be stoned, but when her accusers slip away she is condemned no more and she comes home to her God.

The fact that it would have been a legal stoning is very much the point, and we shouldn't be surprised by the religious leaders' quibbling about the disciples eating corn or about Jesus healing on the Sabbath. This was important. So much of what Jesus and his followers did appeared contrary to the law and therefore, it was thought, contrary to the God who had given the law. Whatever their motivation was for upholding the law – and perhaps some of it was a desire to please, however misguided – the religious leaders were now wallowing in self-righteousness, and they congratulated themselves on having spent a lifetime fulfilling the law in every detail, on having dotted every i and crossed every t. And what an effort it had been! How dare Jesus suggest that God would open his arms to any old sinner and at no cost to the sinner?

This is the older brother. He has done a good job and behaved himself impeccably as a dutiful, respectful and respectable son. Unfortunately, what this has produced in him is an attitude that is self-righteous and judgemental as he looks down on others from his position of moral superiority. Though he would be the last to recognise it, he has assumed his father's role; he is the one who is now dictating the terms. He has failed to understand what it is that his father is doing. In his assumption that rewards have to be earned, he hasn't understood who his father is; he does not know him. In his actions the prodigal son tore apart a relationship which the father has now restored. The older brother, meanwhile, has been living all this time in a damaged relationship which he has no intention of letting anyone restore, not even his father. But he doesn't think that way, so why mend what isn't broken? It's his father who has got it wrong, not him.

I said that this is a scary thing, and it is. It's scary because it is so very easy for any of us to be the older brother. I suspect that some of us have been older brothers all our lives without ever having been the prodigal. Equally, I think it's possible with time for people to move from being the prodigal to a position very close to the older brother's. Even in the church, where our watchword is love, not everybody is living the life of the prodigal, and, sadly, there are sometimes more wagging fingers and furrowed brows than there are parties.

We're talking here about something subtle and insidious. You won't think that you're an older brother, because one of the inevitable results of self-righteousness is that there's nothing wrong with you. It's likely that you could very easily point to older brothers in your congregation, but it's unlikely that you count yourself among them. "I can remember being a prodigal," you say. "I know the date and the time, and I can quote the exact words of my prayer of repentance." Well done, but that doesn't stop you from being an older brother now.

The older brother is muddled about the important issues, notably that his father's love and therefore his own position as son have to be earned. As he angrily points out, he has spent the whole of his life slaving away in the fields, and for what? Just to see his brother splitting up the estate, squandering all his inheritance on drink and girls, and being welcomed back into the family without so much as a cross word. Even the prodigal is surprised! In his wildest dreams the prodigal had only hoped to be taken on as a servant. No wonder the older brother is so angry. What is his father thinking?

No matter how much we know the truth, it doesn't mean that we always live in it. We may know that God's love is freely given and does not have to be earned, but that doesn't prevent us from trying. As prodigals we may have been given the grace to fall upon our knees and say a helpless "thank you", but as older brothers we try, consciously or unconsciously, to make up for it. Bit by bit we nudge and jostle, or are simply carried along to a position that at our conversion would have seemed absurd: we have earned our salvation.

I love the father's response: "Everything I have is yours." And then, I imagine, "So why all the fuss? You don't have to earn my favour or your inheritance. Everything I have is yours. Not *will be*, but *is*. This thing that you are striving towards, breaking your back for, all these brownie points you're collecting, you have it all now. You've always had it. Why should you have to earn it? And why aren't you enjoying it?"

Let's not kid ourselves, we can't earn God's favour. We can simply enjoy his provision, his love and his presence. In a word, him. The prodigal son may have got a lot wrong for a lot of the time, but he's got it right now, and it's the spirit of the prodigal, and not that of his older brother, that we should daily be practising. In my case it doesn't come all that easily, and so I can't help wondering if, like that little girl who caught my attention in church, I couldn't help myself by spending a little more time dancing in the aisle.

THE PRODIGAL SON

The prodigal son
Is given to shrugs,
Has taken drugs,
May still have bugs, unplugs
His iPod, smothers me with hugs.
He sings
Off key, has piercings,
Misses meetings
Frequently, is eating
When he shouldn't be,
Betrays a fleeting
Sneer at seating
So meticulously arranged.
The prodigal giggles
During sermons (which niggles),
Can be fickle, lets trickle
Between his fingers the articles
Of faith, sits high on a wall
Unaffected
By the gravity of it all.
He's iconoclastic,
Overuses 'drastic' and 'fantastic',
Bounces on elastic,
Is made of plastic,
Sports a hat-trick smile,
Has driven
Ten million miles
Both there and back again,
And knows
That for all of this, and more,
He is forgiven.

A PRAYER

Heavenly Father,
Each day, when I come to you,
You welcome me back as your prodigal son.
You have put down everything
And rushed out to meet me,
And daily I rejoice in your welcome.
Father, help me each day to return to you
For your forgiveness, and help me each day
Never to believe that I can earn it.
Keep alive in me the spirit of the prodigal.
Give me the freedom and the willingness to dance:
To dance in my thoughts,
To dance with my body,
To dance in my spirit,
And as I dance, will you remake me,
Turn my mourning into gladness
And my sorrow into your comfort and your joy.

21

Big Brother (2)

Luke 10:38-42

PRACTISING THE SPIRIT OF THE PRODIGAL? THE TROUBLE IS that there is so much in the structure of the modern church which makes this so difficult! In the empire which each fellowship almost inevitably becomes we create an army of workers, of achievers, of doers. We become a busy little hive of older brothers all working ourselves into old age. This isn't all bad, because the church does need to function. The problems come when the functioning becomes the purpose, and it is such an easy trap to fall into. Jesus' friend Martha knew all about that. Somebody had to make dinner, somebody had to clean and somebody had to fuss. And look, there was her sister doing nothing! But Jesus reprimands Martha. Not true, he says, because Mary is doing the better thing. She is dwelling in the presence of her Lord, practising the spirit of the prodigal. Martha, on the other hand, is practising the spirit of the older brother. Her critical and superior attitude gives her away. It will give us away too. Be careful when you find yourself thinking, "I do so much for the Lord; why do so many do absolutely nothing?" Are you being the older brother? Is your church built on older brothers? Is there even room for the prodigal son?

Linked to all this is the older brother's failure to understand his father and what he is doing. Mary, in her time of devotion, sensed something that her sister didn't and she opened herself up to the Jesus of the moment. Martha, on the other hand, had her own agenda. The older brother always has. Be sure about this: if we have our own agenda, God's will be different. Discovering it will not come naturally to us. Our own plans – and they will seem so right – will almost certainly lead us in a different direction. Through Isaiah God tells his people, "Watch for the new thing I am going to do." [Is.43:19] But the truth is that very often we don't see it; we're too busy looking the other way. We're looking where we think God is or where we think he ought to be. We're doing his planning for him. If the Gospel accounts of Jesus, from his birth to his death, do nothing else, they show us that at every turn God does things differently. He really is a God of surprises. The biggest surprise is that we are so slow to grasp that fact. But then, we're older brothers so we wouldn't.

And if we cannot accept our father, we're not going to accept our younger brother so very easily either. Why should we? His list of misdemeanours is as long as our arm, and he doesn't seem so very repentant. Surely, if he means what he says, he won't accept the party; he will be off to the fields straight away, humble himself a bit and start to earn his pardon. It will take some time, of course, and no matter how hard he tries, he'll never quite get to where we are now, but hard work never hurt anyone, did it? New Christians? All right, I suppose, but they have so much to learn, and they bring with them so many of the trappings of their old life. And that enthusiasm of theirs is so very common. Thank God it won't last.

The spirit of judgement is all-pervasive and creeps up on us when we least expect it. I am of all men most guilty. I remember sitting in church one evening a few minutes before the start of the service. I was, as they say, 'preparing myself for worship'. A man came in I hadn't seen before and sat in the row in front, a little to my right. I thought he looked unsettled, somewhat ill at ease. Had he been drinking? He wouldn't have been the first. I began to imagine his background, his family and his present circumstances, and I wondered why he was there in church. By the time we came to small group prayer – he would have to be in my group! – I had him pretty well sorted, and then, when he prayed, he had me pretty well sorted. He prayed fluently and beautifully; his words were a prayer of faith and confidence in a loving, saving God, a God he knew, and, by the sound of it, knew pretty well. I was humbled, and rightly so. Afterwards I wanted to apologise, but I didn't. I suspect my words would only have added insult to injury, and anyway, he disappeared straight away. I never saw him again.

With his heart in the wrong place, it's very doubtful that even before the prodigal's return the older brother enjoyed the life he had. He was used to it, certainly. Doubtless he worked well. His past had gone to plan, his future would do the same and he knew his place in the scheme of things. But it was a joyless life, and there was something missing. He had followed the path of duty, had obeyed the rules, had always done the right thing, had got on well and had earned a place for himself. But was he happy in himself? Big brothers are rarely happy in themselves, they just think they are. It sometimes takes a prodigal's homecoming to bring this to light, although even then they must have the eyes to see it.

How do you see the new people in your church? I don't mean the quiet couple who sit in the corner, who wouldn't say boo to a goose and who disappear during the last hymn. No, you like them; they present no challenge. The ones I'm talking about are the noisy ones, the flag-wavers, the ones who jump up and down, the huggers, the ones who want to hug you! They may have been believers for twenty or thirty years but there is still something of the prodigal about them and it is so very irritating. "Hang on a bit, you're new here, slow down, show a bit more respect. We've been here a while. We know how things are done, and they aren't done like that."

That's the stern, cold, legalistic side of the older brother talking. But there's another side to this too and it's the jealous side. How come my younger brother is having a party and I'm not? I've been a Christian for ages and I've done everything I should have done. I've read my Bible, I've prayed, I've been the most regular attender at church, I've cooked and I've cleaned. I've deserved a party too, plenty of them, but I've never had one. These people are having a party, and it looks like they're having one all the time. It isn't fair!

This is a moment of crisis. Even though we have let ourselves down badly here – and our Father too – all is not lost. He comes out to see us, to persuade us to join in the celebration. "Don't be jealous," he says. "I'm not treating him any differently from you. 'Everything I have is yours.'" How we react to these words will make us or break us, or, if you like, if it breaks us, it will make us. We can stamp our feet and stand our ground, or we can take the brave route of humility, let our Father put his arms around us too and go and join the party. We can be jealous of our church partygoers, or we can open ourselves once again to our Father's love and forgiveness and ask for the grace to live in all that he has for us. He will not let us down. It will mean becoming a prodigal again, but in a sense we need to be a prodigal each time we come to the Father. It's the only way.

ON FIRST SEEING LINCOLN CATHEDRAL

It is strange that just one building can determine
everything about a city. It's possible
for Paris to exist without the Eiffel Tower;
the Opera House does not hold Sydney in its power,
nor would the absence of the Prado undermine
the status of Madrid. But inadmissible
is Lincoln with no cathedral there to crown her.

I saw its towers through the mist one morning
in September, when all the world around was shapeless
and of little substance. The road barely had form.
The trees, ghosts of themselves, appeared and then were gone
as quickly. Rivers, fields and houses (all one in,
it seemed to me, some sort of wilful hiddenness)
escaped again to nothingness. And then the sun

was, as if for the first time ever, and it shone
to the east, on those three towers only, all else
in white still, invisible and unimagined.
This accident of time and space became a kind
of vision, affected most profoundly all I'd done
and would do in that day, made of a few moments
something with larger significance, underpinned

feelings of being beyond, indescribable.
An hour later, standing in that massive nave,
I saw the same bright sun projecting reds and blues
of stained-glass windows on to men and women who,
to their surprise, had now acquired unutterable
beauty, the colours of angels, which dancing gave
a fresh perspective on all things, made all things new.

A PRAYER

Father,
I confess that I have so often
Been judgemental and superior;
I have followed my own agenda
And done your planning for you;
I have been blind to the work of your Spirit
And deaf to the words of your voice;
I have given more importance
To the workings of your church
Than I have given to you,
And now here I am, standing on the outside.
Come out to me again, Father;
Embrace me, as you embrace my brother;
Forgive me, and take me back inside;
Rebuild me, and help me understand
That I too am a child of my Father
And that everything he has is mine.

22

As We Forgive

John 8:1-11; Matthew 18:21-35

I HAVE NEVER CONSIDERED MYSELF A REBEL, BUT WITH age it has become increasingly obvious to me that I don't like being told what to do. And by this I don't mean that I make a habit of breaking the rules, because I don't. I mean that I struggle with imposed conformity. This may well go back to something deep in my childhood that I am still unaware of, but it's there, and on occasion it shows itself. Some of those occasions, I'm sorry to say, are in church.

It is true that Jesus is the Good Shepherd and that the church is his flock, but let's imitate the best things about these images and not the worst, always guarding against the church leader who is a little too controlling and the flock which is a little too docile. I have watched a few televised Christian rallies from overseas, and I have been alarmed to see how important it is to the speaker that their audience should continually show its appreciation of the points made. After each important statement, the speaker says amen, but in reality it is "Amen?" and it requires a response. So heaven help the audience if its response is anything less than fully enthusiastic, because that is clearly unacceptable and means that they now have to say amen again, and this time a bit louder. And then again if necessary. I accept that it's helpful for a speaker to know that the audience hasn't fallen asleep, but I really don't like that sort of thing.

Fortunately for me, I have found that one of the advantages of growing old (and there are plenty of disadvantages) is that I am finding it easier not to conform if I choose not to. So, if after the sermon the vicar asks us to stand for prayer and hold out our hands in an attitude of receptivity to the Spirit, I may or I may not do one or both of these two things. If I think they will be helpful, I do them. If I think that I will only be doing them because everyone else is doing them, then I don't. Occasionally, I don't do them simply from a desire not to conform, which I find has been wonderfully good for me, although, since pride and awkwardness are always lurking around that corner, I do have to be careful. It is important to be true to ourselves, but not if that means being proud or awkward.

I have said all that as a precursor to telling you about an occasion I remember when the speaker asked this question: "Who wants to be like Jesus?" Perhaps predictably, a million hands shot up at once, which I thought was a bit unfortunate for the guy in the corner who had come in for some warmth and a free coffee, and who may have had no idea who Jesus was. But I did know who Jesus was, so what did I do? Well, I didn't raise my hand, and this time it was nothing to do with conformity. It was because on this particular occasion I knew that I didn't want to be like Jesus. As simple as that. I was being honest.

Right then, as I was being honest, I would have liked to pass round a questionnaire to the owners of the million waving hands and ask them why exactly they wanted to be like Jesus. It isn't, when you think about it, the easiest question to answer. It isn't like asking a teenage athlete why he or she wants to be like Usain Bolt or Dina Asher-Smith, and it isn't like asking an amateur landscape painter why he or she wants to be like Constable or Turner. Those questions have obvious answers, and this one doesn't. If you're not sure about this, ask yourself the question now: why do I want to be like Jesus?

For me, and on that occasion, it was very simple: I didn't want to be like Jesus, because Jesus forgives people. I could have had many other reasons, but for me right then it was the forgiveness thing. Jesus forgives people, and there was some forgiving that I didn't want to do. Of course, I had good reason for not wanting to – we all do – but that doesn't stop Jesus from making forgiveness a big deal. Jesus does forgiveness all the time, he talks about it all the time, he's always asking us to do it, and he even brings it into the Lord's Prayer, so we can never escape the importance of it. And then, on the cross of all places, he does it again. When we might have said just about anything else, Jesus says, "Forgive them, Father! They don't know what they are doing." [Lk.23:34] And it's no use saying that it was so much easier for Jesus to forgive than it is for us, because Jesus was a human being too. He was one of us.

I think that the reason forgiveness is so difficult for us is that we really shouldn't have to do it. It isn't like making an apology, which can also be very hard to do, but at least when we make an apology we are the ones at fault. With forgiveness, it is the other person who is the guilty party; we have done nothing wrong, so why should we go out of our way to remedy things? It's not our job to do that. Well, since Jesus says that it is, I am offering here a few things that I have found helpful.

Firstly, *me*. When, in John 8, Jesus says to the woman's accusers that if any one of them is without sin he may throw the first stone, he is talking to me. He is reminding me that although the other person's offence is real (and Jesus doesn't minimise it), my own offences over a lifetime have been every bit as real and (my addition) possibly worse. He is reminding me that when I adopt a position of unforgiveness, I am setting myself up on a moral pedestal built on some very shaky foundations. Even the slightest tremor will see it fall. In other words, I am not as secure as I think I am.

Secondly, *God*. In being unforgiving, we have become the older brother again, gladly accepting the Father's love and care and protection – and forgiveness – but refusing to offer the same to others. In Jesus' parable of the two debtors, the first man is released from his massive and completely unpayable debt but still refuses to release his own debtor from the few pounds owed. It's terrible, but we do the same thing. We concentrate all our attention and all our emotions on some offence done to us, and we forget, as if it had never existed, the massive and completely unpayable debt from which the Father has released us. And let's not forget that God doesn't have to do that. His moral pedestal does not have the shaky foundations that ours has, and Jesus did not have to pay the massive and completely unimaginable price that he paid. But he did.

Thirdly, *the debt*, which, let's be honest, doesn't seem quite as big now that we have reflected for a few moments on the incomparable love of God shown to us in Jesus. And it is the focusing on the debt, rather than the debtor, that I have found helpful. When I think about the debtor, the individual who has offended me, then that person looms large in my mind and I am overwhelmed by negative emotions. However, when I consider the debt, the offence committed, I find it less oppressive and therefore more manageable. My forgiving the other person really means releasing them from their debt to me, and I find it much easier to do this than to try to summon up a pile of positive emotions that simply refuse to show up. I have on one or two occasions released people from their financial debts to me. Nothing massive, you understand, but still it was easier to do than I thought it would be, perhaps because I was releasing somebody from a debt they couldn't pay by letting go of something that I didn't actually have. It's the same here: the offence has been committed and can't be undone, and I am losing nothing by forgiving except a lot of very negative emotions that I am much better without. For me, this releasing of debts has made forgiveness a lot easier. I cancel the debt, just as the Lord has cancelled mine, and I find that my negative emotions towards the other person are much quicker to heal. This doesn't mean that reconciliation has taken place, because that's a different matter. Reconciliation might never take place. The important thing is that I have released the person from their debt to me, and in the process I have myself been released. I have, if you like, become more like Jesus, which means that next time, if there is a next time, I can be a little less determined not to raise my hand in church.

GETHSEMANE

A wind was blowing in the olive trees
Which stood like withered hands set dead
Against the evening sky. Daylight hung in tatters
On the branches of the olive-green trees,
Fluttered wind-whipped, cut into strips like flesh,
And cast into the air. See the white birds
Rise from their cage and, silent, disappear.

Lifetime away, a fisherman shouting
Something to another on a still lake
Somewhere on the other side of the hill;
A donkey tied still to a wooden stake
Rubbing its big, bewildered head against
An unthinking, whitewashed wall that had seen
Something remarkable, a king pass by.
And the night, tight around his cold shoulders,
Came on, as it had to, like a purple robe.

Stay here, keep watch with me – a plea which falls
On ears that will not hear, a troubled look
Which finds nothing but a vague reflection
In their dull eyes, chained to the earth with sleep.
On this rock tiredness lay in twos and threes,
Snored maybe or fidgeted, swore a blind oath
At matters too deep to comprehend.
And the moon, her face big as space,
Skin blotched like a leper's, watched time run dry
Among the olive trees and reproduced herself
A thousand times in pearls of sweat
Which dripped like blood in patterns on the sand.

Yet not my will but yours, he said. His hands,
Engulfed in prayer, assumed the shape
Of childhood recollections – a butterfly,
Eagles, a boat upon the sea, a cup
Large enough to hold the world, at arm's length

Held out and almost imperceptibly
Withdrawn, till it became one with himself.

Dark forms scurried in the thorn bushes, yelped
Like dogs, and through the outstretched branches
Of the olive trees the stars of heaven appeared
And shone about his bowed head like a crown.

A Prayer

Lord Jesus,
You say I should forgive,
But that is hard,
And you know how hard it is.
Help me, Lord, to understand
That your command is only out of love for me,
Because my unforgiving heart
Is not the heart that you desire,
And because I harm myself, and those around,
In giving home to unforgiveness.
Help me, Lord, to follow your example,
To say, "Forgive them, Father...",
To release each person
From the debts I think they owe,
To hand to you my anger and resentment,
To feel them lifted from my shoulders,
And know that I am given,
In wonderful exchange,
Your peace, my health,
And your "Well done!"

23

Keys of the Kingdom

Matthew 16:13-20

IT WAS A SUNDAY MORNING, AND I WAS LYING IN BED thinking. Most people would have been thinking about how they were going to spend their day off, but I was pondering the nature of sin and eternal punishment. My family tell me that I frown a lot. I tell them that there are a lot of things to frown about, and thinking about sin and eternal punishment on a Sunday morning is certainly one of them. My wife would have been thinking, "Did John really say he would take us out for lunch?" And no, I didn't.

I was trying to get my head round big issues like the Fall, and sin, and hell, and I was in a muddle as usual. Then I saw very clearly in my mind a prison cell, and I understood in a moment that it would be more helpful for me not to concentrate on an after-death punishment but on a present imprisonment, and I needed to understand that it wasn't God who had imprisoned me. And then I saw Jesus standing outside the door holding a set of keys, and I understood that Jesus wasn't condemning me, he was releasing me. To him are given the keys of the kingdom, the keys of death and hell, "for God did not send his son into the world to be its judge, but to be its saviour". [Jn.3:17]

The thing is, Jesus has every right to condemn us, but he doesn't want to. He wants to rescue us and give us a place, to which we have no right, in his Father's kingdom. Consider John 8. When Jesus goes to the Temple, a crowd of people surround him, fascinated. Some religious leaders are there too, but they only want to catch him out. They bring in a woman caught in adultery, for which the Old Testament requirement was death by stoning. They bring only the woman and not the man caught with her, and they make her nothing but a pawn in their continuing battle against Jesus. They have no concern for her as a person, and they have no real concern for the law either; they simply want to use both to get rid of Jesus. They think that they have trapped him this time. If he decides against the death penalty, then he is failing to uphold their God-given law. If he decides in favour, then how does that square with all his talk of love and mercy? And the men watch and wait.

They don't have to wait long. Instead of replying one way or the other, Jesus bends down and writes in the sand. We don't know what he writes. Maybe he is addressing each one of the men in turn, revealing their hidden lives as the woman's had just been revealed, or perhaps he is simply creating time and space for people to calm down. "Whichever one of you has committed no sin may throw the first stone at her," says Jesus, and one by one the men slip away. These men want to condemn the woman, though in fact they have no moral right to do so. Jesus, who on two counts has the right to condemn her, chooses not to. Instead, he sets her free, not only from her accusers, but also from her sin. The prison doors have been opened and the woman released. Jesus warns her not to shut herself in any more. "Go," he says, "but do not sin again."

The more I thought about this picture of release from imprisonment, the more the various pieces of the puzzle were coming together. In Isaiah 61, the Messiah is to be one who will "announce release to captives and freedom to those in prison". Hundreds of years later, when Jesus is beginning his ministry, he stands in the synagogue and reads from the same book: "The Spirit of the Lord is upon me, because he has chosen me to bring good news to the poor. He has sent me to proclaim liberty to the captives and recovery of sight to the blind; to set free the oppressed and announce that the time has come when the Lord will save his people." [Lk.4:18,19]

When Jesus finishes reading, he says the unthinkable. He says, "You know this passage I've just read? It was talking about me!" Jesus comes to give sight to the blind and freedom to the captives. The trouble is that it's very easy not to see that you are a captive. You would think it would be obvious, but it often isn't. The woman caught in adultery could see it, and people like Zacchaeus could see it, but it wasn't true of everyone. Many people would have been amazed if you'd told them they were imprisoned. How could that be possible? After all, life was dandy. They had got everything sorted, including God. No wonder their prison cell was hard to see; they had had a hand in building it.

In John 9 Jesus heals a man born blind, saying, "I am the light for the world." Naturally, the man and his parents are delighted. Wouldn't everybody be delighted? Of course not. Jesus had healed the man on the Sabbath, and the Pharisees could not therefore accept that Jesus was of God. The blind man is over the moon; he's jumping around and telling everybody that he's been released! But the Pharisees don't see this at all. Whereas the man was blind and now isn't, the Pharisees are able to see perfectly well, but are blind both to his joy and to the deeper reality at work here. In fact they are furious, and when the man cheekily suggests that maybe they want to be Jesus' disciples too, they curse him. "We are Moses' disciples," they explain. "We know that God spoke to Moses; as for that fellow, however, we do not even know where he comes from!"

If they had listened to Isaiah they would have known. Here Jesus was doing exactly what the Messiah was going to do, but they couldn't see it. Day by day, brick by brick, they had built up around themselves the structure of their lives. This included God, certainly, but a God made according to the very little that they had understood, or misunderstood, and it admitted nothing of the real him, so that we can see what they can't: their beautiful building is in fact a prison block, and they have shut themselves inside. In Luke 10 Jesus rejoices that his disciples have been allowed to see what many have not seen: "I tell you that many prophets and kings wanted to see what you see, but they could not, and to hear what you hear, but they did not." The Pharisees are seeing and hearing it too, but instead of welcoming their rescuer with open arms they are sitting in judgement on him while he is outside with the keys. "We know what's going on," they nod wisely to themselves. "You can't pull the wool over our eyes." Jesus knows what's going on too. "Since you claim that you can see," he says to the Pharisees, "this means that you are still guilty." Because they see nothing at all.

I love this picture of Jesus on his rescue mission. Because he loves me, he has the keys to my prison in his hands, and he wants nothing more than to let me out. An hour or two later on the same Sunday morning, I was in church as usual. There were a million possibilities for the subject of the children's address, so imagine my amazement when our pastor did a tour of the church and collected in a basket everybody's bunch of keys. "I've done this so that you will remember one very important thing," he said. "Jesus is our Saviour, and he has been given the keys of the kingdom." What are the odds of that happening? And, more importantly, which prison doors would I like him to unlock?

JESUS IS

Jesus is my bread and wine
My diamond mine
Top of the line
Cloud nine
My 'This Way' sign

Jesus is my stable ground
My rock
My turn around
Jesus is my lost and found
My ticket on the underground

Jesus is my second chance
And then my third
Lord of the Dance
Of every circumstance
The missing word

Jesus is my saving grace
A strong embrace
Salt tears all down my face
He is my safe
And slowly breathing space

Jesus is my breaking dawn
My rising sun
My race well run
My trophy won
Jesus is my number one
My recreated life begun

Jesus is my yellow brick road
My guiding hand
The cracking of the code
The Promised Land
He is the single line of footprints in the sand

Jesus is my God with us
His make-no-mistake-about-it "Yes!"
Largesse
Finesse
Noblesse
God's "Nonetheless…"

Jesus is my sacrificial lamb
My superhero friend
The Resurrected Man
My beginning and my end
In him I live, and breathe, and move, and am

A Prayer

Lord Jesus,
You say to us, as you said to Peter,
"Who do you say that I am?"
And, in borrowed words, we say,
"You are the Christ, the Son of the Living God.
You are the anointed one,
Who brings good news to the poor,
Who heals the broken-hearted,
Who gives freedom to the captives
And release to the imprisoned."

Come, Lord Jesus, and release us
From all that holds us captive.
Release us from our doubts and our anxieties;
Release us from our fears and our addictions;
And release us from our self-importance,
From that easy way we have of making ourselves
The very centre of the universe.

Thank you, Lord Jesus,
That you have paid the price for our release.
Give us the sensitivity of your Spirit,
To see around us any who might be captive,
And may we have the courage and the willingness
To join with you in opening their prison doors.

24

Putting Out the Bins

Genesis 37; 39-45

IT'S HARD BEING IN THE WRONG WHEN YOU KNOW YOU'RE right. It happened to me this morning with the refuse collection. Today is Saturday, the second of January, and with the Christmas disruption to bin collection I had worked out that today was going to be bin day. Knowing that, I should simply have put the refuse out, but I didn't, because I made the mistake of checking the website first, and that showed a non-bin day. *OK,* I thought, *I'll check the street later,* which I did, but it was dark, and the street was dark, and the bins are dark, and I didn't see any bins at all. *I must be wrong,* I thought, even though I knew I wasn't. And then, at eight o'clock this morning, as I was on the point of thinking about getting up, I heard them coming. I can still move quickly when I want to, and in no time at all I was relatively dressed, out of the back door and dragging my wheelie bin down the street towards a lorry that seemed to be going even faster than I was, and although I tried to pull it quietly, I was probably making enough noise to waken not just my neighbours but also any dead people who happened to be buried nearby.

And so it happens that sometimes we may find ourselves in the wrong when we know within ourselves that we are in the right, and that's an uncomfortable place to be. Joseph was very familiar with it. Spoiled by his father, and afterwards hated, thrown into a pit, very nearly murdered and then sold into slavery by his brothers, Joseph finds himself in Egypt, and he must think, like King Lear, that he is more sinned against than sinning. In Egypt things start to improve, but then Potiphar's wife puts him back in the pit again, this time the palace dungeon, where yet again things improve for a time until the cup-bearer forgets all about him and consigns him to two more years of life down below. That's a lot of negative treatment to handle when it isn't your fault. Similar, if less extreme, things can happen to us too. Perhaps in the family, perhaps at work, and even in the church, we may find ourselves in that difficult place. We have done something or we have said something, we have pointed something out or expressed an opinion, and despite knowing that we were right, in no time at all we find ourselves treated as if we were wrong. If we are fortunate, there will be an enquiry with a genuine attempt to set things straight, but for a number of reasons this might not happen – it didn't happen for Joseph – and then what? What did Joseph do?

Well, he didn't do what we are usually tempted to do: he didn't seek his own vindication, and there are times when for us this is the best example to follow. I am not saying by this that we should never stand up for ourselves, because I don't believe that the Lord wants us to be doormats. But I am saying that there may well be times when attempting to vindicate ourselves will be impossible, or pointless, or will make matters even worse. As hard as it may be, there are times when we simply have to wait until the Lord does the vindicating for us, as he did for Joseph. It may have taken some time, but it was the Lord who raised him up, and he raised him up in ways that Joseph could never have done for himself. And Joseph isn't simply vindicated, he is vindicated *plus*, because it is in the midst of this tale of apparent woe that the Lord allows him to blossom in the gifts he has been given, not just his spiritual gifts of prophetic dreams and their interpretation, but also his vocational gifts of administration and management in which he shines above all those around him.

There is more, because Joseph makes it very clear to his brothers in chapter 45 that God meant it all for good, that God had planned all this from the beginning in order to save his people. Admirably, given the circumstances, Joseph sees his life, including his suffering, as inherent in God's purposes for the greater good of his family and their descendants, and it is clear that without the events of Joseph's life, the story of God's people would have been very different and without its fundamentally important milestones of Captivity, Moses, Passover, Exodus, Covenant, Priesthood, Wilderness, Journey and Promise, things that we now come close to taking for granted in God's developing relationship with his people. God, through Joseph, wasn't simply saving a family; he was establishing his nation.

But in saving the people, God saves Joseph too, because for God we are never simply cogs in a wheel. For one thing God saves Joseph's life, first at the hands of his brothers and then, I'm guessing, from a possible execution after the business with Potiphar's wife. God saves Joseph's relationships too in a world where all other relationships are broken. His emotional reunion with his brothers could not contrast more sharply with that time when they had wanted to be rid of him; it is a deep healing for all concerned. But God also saves Joseph on another level: he saves him from himself. Whilst it is right that Jacob should carry the blame for spoiling his son, Joseph must have been a real pain to have around. His dreams may have been true, but I suspect that the way he put them across might not have had the tact and sympathy it could have had. So Joseph is brought down – not for ever, of course, but long enough to learn the necessary humility. It takes a while though. Even in prison, when he has the opportunity to promote himself via the cup-bearer, he fails and has to stay locked up for another two years. God will not lift him up before God is ready, and he won't do it before Joseph is ready either.

It can be difficult to be a prophet, and it can be difficult to lift your head up and speak a word of truth when you think it needs to be said. And very often the people who really do need to say something are quiet, unassuming people, and they may have bottled it up for so long that when eventually they speak, they don't always come across well. They may be in the right, but their manner may put them in the wrong. If you're a leader look out for such people; this can be hard because they are not likely to be the loudest people around and they almost certainly won't volunteer for committees. They will be there somewhere though, and when you've found them try to have the courage to listen before they embarrass both themselves and you. And if you are one of these people yourself, do all you can to tell the truth with grace and compassion, because even if you are not heard, and even if you have to wait a long time before being vindicated, you will at least be more able to bear your rejection in a state of quiet and godly humility.

If I am to learn some humility myself, I am going to have to be honest with you. The refuse collectors' website was wrong in not having my bin collection on their new calendar, but the reason for this is that they had expected me to see it on their big, flashy page entitled 'Festive Collections', which I had somehow bypassed. So, ironically, we were both right and both wrong at one and the same time. This I discovered only after trundling my still noisy bin back up the street, and I felt wonderfully relieved that instead of a lengthy speech of self-justification, the only words I had said to the very friendly bin man were, "Thank you." I will try to remember that, should this sort of thing ever happen to me again, which I think it probably will.

It seems to be in our nature always to question God's methods and his purposes. But Jesus likens the work of the Spirit to the wind, and although we may know more and more about the wind and can harness at least some of its power, still it remains out of our control. It is at heart a wild thing, its own master, and I rejoice in that.

OCTOBER DAYS

I love those wild October days
When gulls like flimsy supermarket bags
Are blown this way and that,
Are caught off guard,
Are taken by a sudden snatch of wind
And slide surprised down twisting flumes of air,
Wings very nearly unattached.

There is a loss of firmness to the world.
Trees that yesterday were hanging heavy
With all the weight of the long year
Are seized, shaken, uprooted almost
And give the lie to settledness.

Apples can't hold on. They lose their grip, fall,
Crash shocked through leaves and branches,
Roll rosy-cheeked like snooker balls
To find their limpet spot upon the yielding grass.

People walk at various angles to a wind
Which fashions cocktail glasses from umbrellas,
Sucks startled jackdaws up from chimney pots,
Whines along the telephone lines
And whips the street with rain.

Afterwards we pick up pieces, recollect the noise,
The violence, as if an army has passed by
Invisible, though there are footprints everywhere,
Stamped deep in the damp and mushroom-soldiered earth.

A PRAYER

When I cannot hear the words of Jesus
In the words of those who speak for Jesus,
Let me hear Jesus.

When I cannot see the love of Jesus
On the faces of those who shout for Jesus,
Let me see Jesus.

When I cannot see the hands of Jesus
On the arms of those who lift their hands to Jesus,
Let me see Jesus.

When I cannot see the feet of Jesus
On the legs of those who march for Jesus,
Let me see Jesus.

When I cannot see the heart of Jesus
In the eyes of those who work for Jesus,
Let me see Jesus.

When I cannot see the cross of Jesus
On the backs of those who wear the cross of Jesus,
Let me see Jesus.

When I cannot see Jesus
In the lives of those who live for Jesus,
Let me see Jesus.

25

The Right Question

Exodus 19:1-25; Romans 3:23

IF WE WANT THE RIGHT ANSWER, IT IS IMPORTANT THAT we ask the right question. This was brought home to me one evening, as I sat watching *Richard Osman's House of Games*. In one round, the producers had decided that it would be fun to have the questions written not by the usual question setters but by their children. Gyles Brandreth, like me, made the mistake of assuming that the easiest question would be written by the youngest child, so he plumped for Nola, aged three. He was wrong, because her question was: What begins with the letter j? He assumed, again wrongly, that any word beginning with j would be a correct answer, so after considering a few possibilities he decided on 'joy', because what could be better than joy?

He wasn't joyful for long. Scarlett Moffatt, buzzing in very quickly with her own answer, took a much more practical approach; assuming that little Nola was very much like her, she plumped for 'jam'. Amazingly, jam was correct, and there was much amusement all round, including from me. We'll forgive Nola, because she's three, but if the right answer was jam then the right question should have been: What begins with the letter j, is made from fruit such as strawberries, is often spread on toast and scones, and isn't the word used for that wobbly stuff which children eat at parties? Ask the right question and you're more likely to get the right answer.

I was thinking about questions and answers the other day as I was reading several news reports about President Trump having had a conversation with God. A lot of the questions that people asked about this were predictable and along the lines of "Who does he think he is?" or "If you wanted proof that he's mad, why look any further?", but for me these were not the right questions. The right question, at least initially, is, does God exist? If the answer to this is no, then it's true that we need look no further. If God doesn't exist, then he doesn't talk to anybody and Trump was talking to himself. This answer will also be the right answer for the person who *believes* that God doesn't exist, even if he does. If I don't believe that Australia exists on the other side of the world, I am not going to book a month's holiday there. And if you do, I will most probably laugh at you.

But if God does exist, then we have to ask another question: Does he have conversations with people? Coming at this from a believer's point of view, we have to say that it appears that he does. What is the Bible if not the progressive revelation of God to man by means, in large part, of conversation? Abraham is "the friend of God", and God speaks to him, frequently, just as Abraham speaks to God. The people pray and God answers; God speaks and the people respond. Jesus himself spends what appears to be most of his time talking and listening, and why wouldn't he? After all, he calls his disciples friends, and it would be very surprising indeed if we didn't have conversations with our friends. They probably wouldn't be our friends if we didn't speak to them or listen to what they had to say. So the next important question is, does he still speak today? And again our response is, if God is unchanging, why wouldn't he? Given this, we're missing the point when we ask, "Who does Trump think he is, believing that God wants to speak to him?" Much more important is the question that we should be putting to ourselves: Who do I think I am, believing that God does *not* want to speak to *me*? Why would I consider myself to be so very bad or, conversely, so very good?

This brings us, I think, to another important question that may have been lurking inside many of us who do believe that God speaks today, and that is, what on earth was God doing talking to Trump? Trump is not alone in giving us perhaps a long list of reasons for disapproval, but he has certainly been up there with the best of them. Critics and satirists have had almost more material than they could cope with, and I have seen mild-mannered and generous people, those who would normally keep their opinions to themselves, unable to resist a comment or two, or even an expression of a deep feeling of dislike or revulsion. So why would God talk to him?

Romans 3 shows me that it isn't Trump who needs putting in his place, it's me, because as soon as I question God about Trump, God questions me about me. All have sinned, Paul says, and fallen short of God's glory. I want this to be more about Trump than about me. I want to think that it makes a difference to God that Trump may have fallen lower against God's standard than I have. But it makes no difference at all, because God's standard is a straight line, and we've all fallen below it. There are no nice wavy bits to accommodate me on my bad days.

So, when I ask why on earth God would talk to Trump, Trump could quite legitimately look in my direction and ask exactly the same question about me. If he knew me well enough, he probably would.

In Exodus 19 a boundary line is drawn to keep the Israelites from approaching the mountain of the Lord too closely. The Temple too had boundary lines, the most important being the curtain to the holy of holies. In both cases, and with one or two special exceptions, the people of God were not to approach the presence of God; they had to stay on the side of the line where they belonged. Here again we might be tempted to ask the wrong question: Isn't God awful, looking down on us so much that he can't even bear to be near us? But in Romans 3 Paul helps us to arrive at right question, which is something like: Isn't God good, sparing us from being burned up in his presence? It is God's glory, says Paul, that we have fallen short of, not simply his law. It isn't just that God's standard is different, *everything* is different. His nature is different. He is altogether other.

A few evenings ago I had to go to the bottom of the garden to get something from the shed. It was already dark, but not so dark that I could not safely make the round trip. Street lights provided something of a glow, and a chunk of moon was doing its best to push through cloud. There was light enough for me. However, once back in the house, I looked outside to where I had just been. There was an impenetrable blackness, and it was difficult to imagine that the two things had happened in the same few moments. Or in the same world.

Unaccompanied, we cannot enter the brightness of God's glory or we will be burned up. But in Jesus a light enters the darkness, and in humility and grace the glory of the Lord comes to us. "I will be like you," says Jesus, "so that you can be like me, and then we can go into the presence of our Father together." In a world filled with questions, it's good to know that we can rest, knowing that all the answers are summed up for us in him, Jesus, the Light of the World.

QUESTIONS

As the green grass shoots, and buds blossom,
I feel again the breath of God
Upon this land, in the still air,
In the quiet yet insistent drone
Of bees, buzzing in blooms open
To possibilities, and to them.

But if it is that God inhabits
Such spring rebreathing, why not say too
That his must be the breath that chills
Our winter bones, sets icy teeth
On edge along the hanging eaves, and freezes
Coffin-hard the ground beneath our feet?

And were this taken from us, were
Our sturdy summer crops to fail,
And grapes to wither on their vines, why say
That God's life-giving breath had ceased,
Should earth crack, and skies weep, and winds
Blow furious across a sea of sand?

A Meditation before My Heavenly Father

When I wonder if my existence – and the existence of this planet I'm stuck to – is nothing more than a cosmic accident, I am reminded that you created all things, simply because you wanted to, simply because it pleased you to do so. For reasons I cannot fathom, you take pleasure in me.

When I wonder if I am alone in the universe, I am reminded that in Christ I am your child, loved with a love that will outlast the sun, the stars and whatever lies beyond them.

When I wonder if my life has any meaning, I am reminded that I have been called according to your purposes to live the life of your Son and to allow him to be glorified in me.

When I wonder if I am worth nothing, I am reminded that however true that may feel, there is nothing that can separate me from your love in Christ Jesus, nothing in worlds visible or invisible or even imagined. I am reminded that you alone are worthy and that I find my worth in you. As Jesus is, so too I am infinitely precious to you.

When I wonder if what I have done is unforgivable, I am reminded that if I confess my sins you are faithful and just, and will forgive me and purify me from wrongdoing.

When I have drifted, and when I wonder if it's possible to find a way back, I am reminded that the Good Shepherd leaves his ninety-nine sheep at home and goes out to find the one that is lost. And when he finds it, he throws a party for all his friends and neighbours. And for the sheep too.

When I wonder why there are difficult times, I am reminded that this is only what Jesus promised and that by thinking something different I have simply been deceiving myself. "But don't worry," he said. "I have overcome the world." Which means that I can too.

26

Thanks a Lot

Luke 17:11-19; Psalm 50:7-15

TAKE AN AVERAGE DAY AND IN IT CONDUCT A LITTLE EX-periment. Do two things. One, in every conversation that you have, count how many times the other person (a) moans and (b) expresses gratitude. Two, do the same with your own words and thoughts.

I may be wrong to prejudge the results, but I have a good idea of the way things will go. Firstly, those you meet are more likely to offer a grumble than a vote of thanks. Secondly, you will probably do the same yourself. It may be an illness peculiar to the British, but we'd rather bemoan the rainfall than welcome it, and even if it isn't raining it is much more probable that we will describe the weather not as good but as "not bad".

A discussion of our physical state often produces similar results. "How are you?" we ask. "Not bad," says the other person, "*all things considered.*" That would be a good answer. We might also hear, "I've been better," "All right under the circumstances," "Bearing up," or even, "It's downhill from here." A good one to tick off the list is the enigmatic "You know", said with a slight shrug of the shoulders. No, I don't know, that's why I'm asking. Mind you, what's even worse is people telling you how they are even though you haven't asked.

A significant problem with the complaining attitude is that if we let it, complaining can become the person we are. During the seven years I was in my last job, one of my colleagues (who worked only five hours a day and finished at 2.30 p.m.) invariably went out of the door with the words "Thank God that's over!" Curious about this, I asked how long she had been working there. "Over thirty years," came the reply. Imagine, thirty years of thanking God that each working day was over. Another colleague, whilst not exactly rejoicing in her work, took the rather more acceptable "It could be worse" approach. For example, "I could now be starting a twelve-hour shift down a Siberian salt mine." Which, given different circumstances, I suppose she could have been, and it really would have been worse.

Having focused recently on my prayer list, what I did the other day (and somewhat by accident, I'm afraid) was to look at my answered prayer list. I'm in the habit, when I remember, of ticking off prayers when God answers them, and what I hadn't noticed until then was just how many ticks there were. And something else I hadn't done was to make much of a point of saying thank you. I'd been faithful in my praying (well, a bit faithful) but not very faithful in my thanking.

According to Luke's account of Jesus' healing of ten lepers, I have at least nine others to keep me company. Their request (their prayer, if you like) wasn't mumbled or half-hearted. They shouted to Jesus, and they had to, because their leprosy made them ritually unclean, so their uncleanness had put them at a distance in more ways than one: they weren't only sick, they were apart. Jesus puts all that right with a word of command, and as the ten men do what they're told, they find themselves healed, and clean, and back in the fold. But even Jesus, who knows better than anyone the hearts of men, is amazed that only one of them comes back to thank him.

This suggests to me that something very important is going on in this giving of thanks. Why, for example, does Jesus say to this healed Samaritan, "Your faith has made you well"? Wasn't he already healed, or has something deeper happened in this second exchange? The other nine were healed and they were made ritually clean, and then they might have thought, "That's it, two out of two. All's well with the world!" But the Samaritan was stirred to do something more, to give thanks, and although he would have been unaware of it, he was proving that the perfect score wasn't two out of two but three out of three, this third thing being a cleansing not of the body, and not in the sphere of ritual, but in the realm of the spirit. The other nine had got what they wanted, and twice over. The Samaritan received something even more precious: he got relationship with God.

It seems that when we come to the Lord, the password is "Thank you", and Psalm 50 points us in the same direction. Here God explains to his people that although they are not doing wrong by offering their dutiful and abundant sacrifices, what he longs for is their thanksgiving sacrifice: "Let the giving of thanks be your sacrifice to God." In other words, we may be ritually clean but still have hearts far from God. We may also be ritually unclean (the Samaritans were considered to be even lower than that) but have hearts brimming over with thanks and devotion. It's clear which God prefers. Ritual is not wrong, but it can lead all too easily to little more than form, appearance and, heaven help us, respectability. It can close the door of the heart. The good thing about giving thanks is that it opens up our closed hearts and enables relationship to be restored. No wonder Paul encourages us to give thanks always. If we do, we are much more likely to be able to do that other thing that he urges: have praise in our hearts. And so, how about a new resolution? We will, from today, do our utmost to make thankfulness a way of being.

One Sunday morning in prayer ministry, we found ourselves praying again with Sarah, she of the credit crunch. It had been a year since our previous meeting. "No requests this time," she said. "I simply want to give thanks to God for his faithfulness to us over the past twelve months." So we did, and it felt so good.

I THANK YOU THAT THE RED LEAF FALLS

I thank you that the red leaf falls
I thank you that the moorland curlew calls
I thank you that the shallow puddle fills
I thank you that the rainbow thrills

I thank you that the blushing poplar burns
I thank you that the screeching swift returns
I thank you that the scented pine trees stand
I thank you that the summer days expand

I thank you that the mountain stream begins
I thank you that the tiny spider spins
I thank you that the silver wood-smoke drifts
I thank you that the salty shingle shifts

I thank you that the owl in winter hoots
I thank you that the fragrant hyacinth shoots
I thank you that the Orange-tip emerges
I thank you that the April shower purges

I thank you that the singing skylark rises
I thank you that the hoverfly surprises
I thank you that the morning mist conceals
I thank you that the mid-day sun reveals

A PRAYER

I thank you, Lord,
For this moment of morning stillness
And for all it holds, here
And now in this quiet space:
The ticking clock which hands out time
Enough for prayer; the sun, lifting over near roofs,
That plays with shadows on the chimney breast;
One hundred daffodils for Mother's Day
That jostle for position by the fire, wrestling
In shape and colour next to dusty purples
Of last summer's lavender. I thank you, Lord,
For all these gone-unnoticed things:
How this orchid flower, in peach, gazes
Open and searching, like the face of Mary
To the angel, and how the small, wooden cross,
Made by a child in school, stands unassuming,
And lets pass by, almost, that its Jesus, resurrected,
Holds all these lovely things close to himself,
Just as he holds this moment, and this me.

27

Dying in the Desert

Exodus 16

I LEFT TEACHING SHORTLY BEFORE MY FIFTIETH BIRTH-day. I wish I could say that life was plain sailing after that, but it wasn't. A lot of it was hard, and there were times when, like the Israelites, I said, "Lord, why have you brought us out here to die in the desert?" And that's odd, because I still thought that the decision I made was the right one.

Doubtless thanks to my own lack of motivation, I didn't have another job lined up, somehow believing that one would fall from the sky and land in my lap. This meant that for several months I was engaged in temporary employment, first in a factory, packing vacuum cleaners, and then with a cold storage firm as office boy. "Lord," I said, "why did you bring me here to die in these places?" In other words, I blamed God for it.

The circumstances of life can fill us with such frustration that if we don't release it we'll burst. It's then that it's as well to let God have it; he's big enough to deal with it, and we're not. But this isn't the same as blaming him. When we blame him, we are rewriting the past and living in a present that is equally untrue. "Why did you make me leave my job?" I complained. "Why did you bring us up out of Egypt to die in the desert?" grumbled the Israelites. And God hadn't done either of those things. The trouble is that our blaming God produces a distortion in our perception of him, and this leads to a lack of faith, because our interpretation of both the present and the past shows that God must be unreliable. "...to die in the desert," say the Israelites, ignoring the fact that God's promise was not to kill them but to lead them to a land flowing with milk and honey. When you blame God for something, you can be sure that you have already begun to twist what you've heard him say, and you can be certain that you don't trust him as much as you did before.

So, having blamed God for my predicament, I followed the Israelites into nostalgia. It appears that it was so bad in the desert that they wanted to return to Egypt, and this was another distortion of the truth, because Egypt wasn't a place where they had been enjoying a holiday at Sharm el Sheikh, lying on sunbeds and diving over reefs. Egypt was where they had been slaves and where their children had been thrown into the Nile at birth. Egypt was somewhere they couldn't wait to get out of, but now all they could think of was a plate of Egyptian stew.

I did the same, and three months into my new life I was interviewed at a neighbouring school for a temporary job, which I got. "Aha!" I said. "The Lord wants me back in teaching." But maybe he didn't, because I spent the next two terms remembering painfully exactly why it was that I'd left in the first place. At the end of the summer I was telephoned by the headmaster at the school I had left only a year earlier. A colleague had left through ill health, and could I fill in? "Aha!" I said again. "The Lord *does* want me back in teaching." But maybe he didn't, because after only one year I felt like a fish out of water. I had gone back but not to the same place; both the school and I had moved on. My mind had been playing tricks on me again.

The Israelites had moved on too, and what they had moved on to was better, but in some ways much scarier than where they had been before. Where they were now was in a place of complete and daily reliance on God. We sometimes say very glibly that with God we can only live one day at a time, but it's true. God assures us of his presence with us tomorrow, and into the future, but he won't tell us what either tomorrow or the future are going to bring. What he wants is for us to live with him in the now. We cannot escape this. When Moses meets God in the burning bush, God gives his name: I am. The Israelites are taught this every day: God provides only enough manna for one day at a time. There is new provision for each day only, and the Israelites are made to understand this. Left to their own devices, madly stocking their larders, they would never have taken that in. The words of Golda Meir, former prime minister of Israel, seem relevant here: "Let me tell you something that we Israelis have against Moses. He took us forty years through the desert in order to bring us to the one spot in the Middle East that has no oil." Exactly.

So did it work out for me? Yes, I think so, though I felt that on most days I was still wandering with the Israelites in the desert, more or less content to live one day at a time but uncertain as to where I was going. But we were provided for, and daily there was enough. In fact that's not true, because there was *more* than enough. After the two schools experience I was back to temping for a while, but then I took up an office job where I remained for over seven years. Did God provide it? I don't know, but the office was one hundred yards from my house, and I didn't apply for the job; it was offered to me by an agency. Ironic, isn't it, that the position where I spent the largest amount of time was the one right next to where I live and that I didn't know was available? I once asked my wife what she would say if I were again offered a full-time teaching job. She said, "I'd tell you not to take it. I prefer you the way you are now."

DESERT SONG

Distances between everything but sand are very long.
That land we left behind seems no more of this life;
Impossible even to imagine, this side
Of death, that home we travel slowly on towards.
I kick at stones. Reluctant, they move a little, but change
Nothing more than place, and then resume their mime,
Smooth-faced, impassive, sitting out eternity
Beneath a sun permitting neither smile nor frown.
We are between worlds, grit in the backs of our eyes,
Skin pinned tight on frames of bleached bone.
Did we really watch the water part? Did my feet
Walk dry on ground that we had been the first to see?
And that release we felt, that lightness of spirit
As we kissed that new shore, stepped out
Hopeful, in a way reborn, ready to run,
Prepared to follow anyone, or anything, to anywhere.
But can I peg my wandering life to a cloud of dust?
Can I chase lights that flicker and fall
Into the well of a bottomless night?
Give me, instead, my mirage of palms
And palaces that each day rides
Like a sand ship on waves of the liquid sky.
Or let me dream again of morning dew,
Sprinkled on the earth like bread flakes,
And of flocks of birds, freshly fallen,
Plump and ripe for plucking.

A Prayer

Jesus,
I do not see clearly where I am heading,
And I cannot, with any certainty, say
Where it is that I have been;
Even in this present moment there is mystery.
But I know this: that you are,
And that you have been,
And that you will be
In all this with me;
That you never leave me,
Neither do you forsake me,
And always you bring me back
To our heavenly Father, who delights
In making perfect sense of all things.

28

Grieving Over Saul

1 Samuel 15:10-16; 16:1-13

I'VE WATCHED A COUPLE OF THOSE PROGRAMMES ABOUT compulsive hoarders. On the upside they made me feel good about myself; although I keep more than I need to, at least I know where the phone is. The downside is that their hoarding had ruined these people's lives. They were trapped – inside their homes, inside their heads and inside the past. To an observer, the hoarder has a serious problem, but to the hoarder this clutter makes perfect sense: "You never know when it might come in useful." And though they may admit that things aren't quite right, it's only with the help of others that they can begin to throw out and, in an emptier house, live a fuller life. Less really is more.

But what if I'm wrong with my 'them and us' attitude? Maybe there's a bit of a hoarder in all of us. I have, still, my first *Encyclopaedia of Animals*. It is completely out of date, lives in a box in the attic and smells mouldy, but I shall probably hang on to it, even though my children will take it to the tip as soon as I'm gone. After all, it has sentimental value, and when our emotions are involved our things are even harder to get rid of. I suspect it happens to all of us at one time or another. It certainly happened to Samuel.

"How long will you go on grieving over Saul?" asks God, and I think that God is asking me the same thing. How long will I go on grieving over events that I cannot go back and change, over past failures and disappointments, over things that didn't work out in the way that I'd planned or hoped? How long will I go on grieving over times when I let people down or when they let me down? How long will I go on rehearsing those times, wishing I could live them again but this time differently? How long will I go on saying, "If only..."?

This grieving can be particularly keen if we are grieving over something that we believed God was involved in. We had a vision, we had specific guidance, we were obedient to a call, perhaps God even spoke our name. God was in it, we knew that, but somehow it didn't turn out in the way it was meant to, and now we're finding this failure very difficult to bear. It's making us question the call. It's making us question God. In fact it's making us question everything. We're stuck in the past, going over events again and again, revolving around the same spot like a hamster in a wheel. We are so absorbed in it that although we know we need help, we can't lift our heads to ask.

Nevertheless, God helps. He tells us to get over it, which at first may seem a bit harsh until we realise that he's had to do the same thing himself. "I am sorry that I made Saul king," says God to Samuel, and God grieves, almost certainly more deeply than Samuel does. But it wasn't God's fault that Saul failed; Saul failed through disobedience and pride. God *had* been in it from the beginning, and Samuel *had* heard the call correctly. The fact that things had gone wrong wasn't the fault of either of them, so Samuel can now stop his grieving, as God has done. And he certainly has no need to do God's grieving for him, which I suspect he has been doing, just a little.

The second way in which God picks Samuel up is to reaffirm him in his call. In one sense, it's a bit more of the same tough love, because Samuel is immediately scared for his life. But it's the very best thing for him. Samuel was judge in Israel and he had anointed Israel's first king. Now God tells him to go and anoint the second. Self-absorption in our grieving will keep us from doing a lot of the things that God has called and equipped us to do. Giving up our grieving will allow him to call us again. It may frighten us at first, but we should do it, because in exercising our call we discover who we really are.

There's one more lesson here for Samuel. In his grieving, Samuel will have been blaming himself for much of what went wrong with Saul. In other words, he has exaggerated his role in the events; there has been a little too much self-importance. Fresh in his new call, Samuel immediately makes the same mistake. As soon as he sees Jesse's eldest son, presumably tall, handsome, strong and king-like, Samuel assumes that he must be the one. He judges again according to his own eyes, and God has to put him straight – again. When the second son appears, Samuel gets it right, because this time he puts himself to one side and listens to the voice of God. God, he realises, is in charge of events, even those events in the past that seemed such a muddle, so he might as well trust him to have his way now.

A couple of days after writing the above, I had a vivid dream. I was back in one of my previous places of employment, and it was my leaving day. The strange thing was that I was saying goodbye without having cleared out any of my things. Other members of staff stood around in amazement, seeing my cupboards brimming over with papers and books. The next day I prayed about this and acknowledged the truth that I believed was contained in the dream: I was still grieving about having left. A couple of weeks later I had another dream. This time I entered the same building by the front door, walked along the dimly lit corridor and opened the door of the room where I had worked. There was nobody else there, but the lights were on. I looked around the room, put my hand on the light switch and very calmly turned it off.

NIGHT LANDINGS

Now, in the autumn of my days,
I watch with some unease
The lines of rooks that in late afternoons
Come past like war planes through
My narrow air space, off to roost
In places scratched, now, from my still-to-visit list.
Without my willing it, without even
Some acquiescence on my part, these birds
Are drawing early evenings across the sky.
I sense that life is straitening somewhat.
Urgency rubs shoulders with detachment,
Jostles for position; so much and more
Still to be done, so little room available
For casual manoeuvres in a wide road.

A little later now, and more appropriate
Somehow, I stand in quiet admiration
Of starlings shoaling over Sainsbury's.
Bait balls of ink, they mock in the pink sky
The supermarket's unambitious lines,
Its token trees, the brassy neon signs,
And rise above it all, their unpredictable
Designs provoking in me something like awe.
Now visible, now gone, momentarily,
They reappear elsewhere, shape shift, split apart
Then coalesce, dip, lift up again, put off
For now today's inevitable landing.
Unfailingly they take me by surprise,
Unnerve me, question my rootedness,
Challenge, so gracefully, the form I have assumed
And worn so heavily. Quite unintentionally
They make a thing of beauty out of nothing:
The simple act of settling for the night.

A Prayer

Father, I thank you that when I have grieved over my disappointments, you will not allow me to wallow in them for ever. I thank you that you encourage me to look up, to see the new thing that you are doing, the fresh shoots that spring up all around me. I thank you that you haven't finished with me yet, and never will, and that even now you have a new commission for me. All you ask is, "Are you willing?" And I say, "Yes, Lord. I am."

29

Heart's Desires

Exodus 3

WHEN MY YOUNGEST DAUGHTER WAS STILL IN HER TEENS, some friends invited her to their church. She went along and liked it. I asked her afterwards if there were many other young people there. "Yes, lots," she replied, "and they were just like you and me, Dad." "In what way?" I asked. With no hesitation she came back at me, "They were all sitting around waiting for God to tell them what to do."

This delighted me; it was evidence of my daughter's growing powers of perception. But it disappointed me too, because even in this new and in many ways exciting church, young believers were still falling into the same trap. But who am I to complain? It's a trap I've fallen into more times than I care to remember, so that this trap and I are almost the same thing. When people see me, I imagine they must be saying, "Ah, here's John. By the look on his face he's still waiting for God to tell him what to do." They are not always wrong.

Experiences in my post-teaching period have suggested to me that 'God having a plan for my life' doesn't mean what I once rather narrowly thought it meant. Convinced that I had been in my job long enough, I decided to quit, and free from the confines of that particular work, I devoted some time to listening for the voice of God as to my future. I heard nothing. In the end I had to take work at random in order to pay the bills, and I wasn't pleased. "I've made myself available," I explained to a friend, "in a way that few people do, and I'm none the wiser. In many ways I'm worse off." My friend's eyes twinkled. "So God's missed his chance, has he?" Truth is, at that time I thought that maybe he had.

When sitting around waiting for God to tell me what to do wasn't working, I searched the Bible in order to find people who, like me, were sitting around waiting for God to tell them what to do. You'd imagine it would be full of them, but I found the opposite. When God spoke to people and told them what he wanted them to do, they were usually happily doing something else. Many of them, in the Old Testament in particular, heard God's voice and definitely wished they hadn't. They didn't want God's plan for their lives before they heard it, and after hearing it they were even more certain they didn't want it.

Moses wasn't in the desert waiting for God's divine plan for his life; he was there tending his sheep. He was trying to keep his head down, not attempting to stick it above the parapet. It wasn't simply that God's presence in the burning bush and his plan for the freedom of Israel through Moses weren't what Moses was expecting; he wasn't expecting *anything.* He wanted to be left alone, and when he had met the Almighty God, and in a way that no man had met him before, and heard this most fantastic of plans, he wasn't all that impressed. He still wanted to be left alone. He wanted to get back to his sheep.

I thought too of Gideon, hiding in his wine press for fear of the Midianites. Was he waiting there for God to unfold the plan for his life? I doubt it. His people had prayed, certainly, begging God to rescue them, but Gideon definitely wasn't waiting for the top job. What about Jeremiah? God comes to him, saying, "...before you were born I selected you to be a prophet to the nations." Does Jeremiah jump for joy? Not at all. "Sovereign Lord," he answers, "I don't know how to speak; I am too young." In other words, "Get me out of here!" And Jonah? He's so quick to scarper in the other direction that I don't think he'd spent years opening himself up to the perfect will of God. But the perfect will of God had found him, and there was no escape.

There was no escape for me either. It just so happened that around this point I was reading Ronald Dunn's *Don't Just Stand There... Pray Something!*, and he makes the very same point: it is God's responsibility to reveal his will and to reveal it in a way that we can't miss it. I had the feeling at this point that I was being spoken to. How come, I wondered, I hadn't heard this message as clearly before? How come so many people still need to hear it? And if it's true, what do I do now?

I'm resisting making generalisations about all this, because I know all too well that 'guidance' is a broad and sometimes tricky area, so I'm going to offer no more than a few observations. Firstly, whilst it is good and right to seek the Lord's involvement and guidance in my decisions, it might very often be better if I sought them on my feet, prepared to take at least one step along a possible path, rather than making no attempt to rise from the comfort of my garden hammock. Secondly, it's also important to recognise that God might reveal his will in what I am tempted to consider insignificant areas of my life. The fact is that we can come to see God's will as concerning only the big things like marriages, jobs and homes. What if the opposite is just as likely to be true? What if in the course of each day, whoever we're married to, whatever job we're doing and whichever house we're living in, God is trying to get through to us about a hundred other things and we never notice? If this is true, then these things are at the top of God's priority list, even if they are so far down ours that we don't know they're there. We'd like to have a big call, and we think, "If I'd been Moses at the burning bush I would have jumped at the offer." But we wouldn't, because when God speaks to us now we don't jump up wildly at the sound of his voice. Let's be honest, we hardly ever hear it. "Give me an important job," we say, and God says, "I'm trying to, but your important and my important are clearly not the same thing." Being sensitive to the voice of God is not something that comes naturally to most of us. We say, "But your voice was so quiet, Lord. Is it our fault we didn't hear you?" And God asks us why, even allowing for that, we haven't carried out his will as revealed in his word. If we're so bothered about knowing his will for our life, why have we not even begun to do all those things that we know he wants us to do, like being a friend or caring for others?

It can be a big temptation to want to be a great Christian. Even the disciples argued about who would be the most important in heaven, and when our Lord says to us one day, "Well done, you good and faithful servant!" we hope he'll say it loud and clear. But who are the greatest Christians you know? For me they are some very ordinary men and women who have taken seriously God's words about loving and caring for others, people who visit the sick when they could be on the beach, those who bring elderly people to church, and those who get up during a church service to fetch a glass of water for someone with a cough when I pretend I haven't heard it. I have a feeling that being a good and faithful servant is as much to do with things like this as it is with having the big appointment. Maybe more.

And these people do ordinary jobs. I doubt if they've ever sat around wondering about God's plan for their lives; they've just got on with it. Getting on with it is important, because one of the dangers of sitting around waiting for the voice of God is that we do nothing. We are neither salt nor light to anyone. These people I'm talking about are salt and light wherever they are, even in jobs to which they have felt no special calling. They are playing the hand of cards they have been dealt, not sitting looking at their cards and wondering what on earth they are.

Of course, jobs are important. I've come to doubt, though, that in general God is as bothered as I thought he was about which one we do, except, and here's the third thing, I think we'll be happiest in it if it's one to which we are suited and where we can best use our gifts. How can we know? By looking inside ourselves and doing what proves hard for many: knowing our heart's desires, our passions and our talents. Those who have no awareness of God can be good at this, but Christians desperate to please their heavenly Father are not always good at knowing what their heart desires and may even think that their heart shouldn't desire anything. And here I'm not talking about wanting to win the lottery, I'm talking about those deep desires whose realisation allows you to be the real you, at ease with yourself and those around you, fulfilling the gifts and the potential wrapped up in you. I don't say it's easy, and it may need practice, but I suspect that learning to hear the voice of our own heart is a step towards hearing more easily the voice of our Father in heaven.

Alex, a pupil of mine in his final year, was going through the university application process, though I felt very strongly that university was not for him. He was unshakeably stuck on criminal psychology, a course I was pretty certain he had no chance of getting on to, so I asked Alex to stop talking, to stop thinking and to shut out anything other than his deepest desires with regard to a career in the big bad world. I half expected a protracted silence; a lot of young people don't know what to say when you ask them a question like that. But not Alex. Quick as a flash he said, "I'd become a professional diver." Bingo!

WHERE WERE THE SIGNS, LORD?

Where were the signs that I missed, Lord,
When I stood in a line to enlist?
I was promised a personal plan, Lord,
But of what was it meant to consist?

Things haven't turned out as I'd pictured
From that sermon on John's revelation.
Was there a sign in a song by Cliff Richard?
Did I join an unspiritual congregation?

Where were the signs, Lord, where were the signs,
Among thousands of clamouring voices?
Where were the signs, Lord, where were the signs,
When it came to those life-changing choices?

I was there with each cry of Hosanna,
I've unpicked with my eyes every banner;
But I find myself worried to pieces
By my doubts on the rightness of fleeces.

My friend found a word in Philemon
On precisely which bus he should take;
A new commentary on Paul gave to Simon,
A baker, advice on which doughnuts to make.

But I've scoured in vain a fine summer sky
For a clue as to just where my pathway should lie;
And I've given the greatest importance to dreams:
I'm a mole in a hole, so it seems.

Where were the signs, Lord, where were the signs,
For my possible change of employment?
To be honest, some clarity just might have helped,
For uncertainty brings no enjoyment.

I've found nothing in theses on predestination;
Heard not a word from old Calvin and co.
Some promise answers from deep meditation,
But that ain't necessarily so.

Head spinning, I haven't known which way to look;
My brain's in perpetual motion;
And I've certainly read about guidance in books,
Though of course by the wrong theologians.

So, supposing the spot where I am now
Is the place where you want me to be,
I'll accept it, I'll love it, with just one proviso,
Please give me a sign I can see!

A Prayer

Let me walk in your ways, Lord.
Let me be a salt that preserves
And a salt that flavours;
Let me be a light that shines
And gives glory to my Father in heaven.

Let me walk in your will, Lord.
Let me hear your voice that guides
And your voice that cautions;
And no matter where I am, or who I'm with,
Let me reveal the heart of Jesus.

Let me walk in your gifts, Lord.
Let me not minimise the gifts I have
Or covet those I don't have;
Let me live true to your design, and see
Your spirit of creation come alive in me.

30

Wanting More

John 5:1-18

THE WORLD IS DIVIDED INTO TWO SORTS OF PEOPLE: THOSE who enjoy camping and those who don't. I remember sitting in a campsite in the Vendée. We'd just finished breakfast, the sun was shining, swallows were dipping in between the trees, and from the top of a pine a wood-pigeon cooed his familiar lament: "My shoes hurt, they do!" Mine didn't, and neither did anything else, because this was just what holidays were meant to be. I picked up my mug of tea from the ground. Tiny ants raced around the rim, a piece of grass floated on the surface, and it was UHT milk, but I didn't care. I only thought how good it all was, and how it seemed much more real than life at home. I said to Carol, "Things are better when you're camping." "Yes, they are," she replied, "and worse."

She was right, of course, not suffering from the delusions that seem a permanent part of my make-up. There have been times when camping has made things much worse. I remembered our holiday in the Auvergne when rain clouds sat on our tent for the whole week, allowing me to learn as if by magic all the three-letter Scrabble words containing x or z, and I thought of the numerous occasions when my sleep has been disturbed by loud noises of all descriptions. I knew too that when you are camping with children, everything takes ten times longer than usual, so that by the end of the day you realise that despite your many plans, you have ended up doing more or less nothing at all.

Now, in a way that's all right. If holidays are a break from the norm then doing nothing is perhaps the very best thing to do. However, I'm one of those people who feel better if at the end of the day I believe I've done something. The problem is that given the nature of the camping experience, I never have much energy for doing anything, so that when by lunchtime Carol asks me what I want to do for the rest of the day, my decision-making capabilities, not good at the best of times, are as ready for action as our groundsheet. "I don't know," I say. "What do *you* want to do?"

I am the master of indecision, even of inertia. Lots of us suffer from it; we'd rather not, but we do. The fault is mine, but in part it stems, I think, from a failure to understand the importance of exercising our own will and not simply the importance of knowing the will of God. I'm not sure how, and I'm certain it's taken the best part of my life, but I have developed the habit of expecting God to make all my decisions for me, and of course I've got a lot of that wrong. There's a story, doubtless apocryphal, about a young man who visited his priest for some advice. "I have a real interest in Peru," he said, "and I'm thinking of spending some time out there, exploring the country and then working with a mission I have contact with in Lima." The priest thought this an excellent idea for all sorts of reasons. "On the other hand," said the young man, "that would cost a pretty penny, and so I was wondering whether it might not be better to donate the entire sum to charity, perhaps to an orphanage over there." "That's also an excellent idea," said the priest, and he gave the young man another set of reasons for thinking so. At this the young man frowned and scratched his head, and then after a short pause he asked, "So, Father, which one should I do?" "Well," replied the priest, "if I have to tell you which one to do, don't do either of them."

Not unconnected, I think, is John's account of the healing at the pool of Bethesda. A lot of sick people were there, believing that when from time to time an angel stirred the water, the first person into the pool would be healed. A man who had been ill for thirty-eight years was among them, and it was this man that Jesus approached. We read in verse 13 that the man did not know who Jesus was, so we don't have the more usual request for healing from the sick person. Instead, it is Jesus who asks the first question, and look at what it is: "Do you want to get well?"

Think about how strange that question is. We might have assumed it was obvious that he wanted to get well, but Jesus sees something else. Does he see that this man's heart's desire has grown weak, that he is resigned to his lot and that the fire has gone out of him? It's been so long now, and why should anything change? Besides, after a while it's easier to have few expectations; if you hope for little, you won't be disappointed – not like those first few times when other people were healed and this man wasn't. It's not surprising then that when Jesus throws this unlikely question at him, the man evades the issue, explaining that nobody is ever there to help him into the water. It's a very adult response. He has looked at all the angles and weighed everything up. It's not his fault; there simply isn't anybody there to help him. He has detached himself. He isn't even sure now what the correct response is. "I don't know. What do *you* want to do?"

I think Jesus would have preferred an emphatic "Yes!" Jesus doesn't want us to be detached; he wants us to be involved and desiring. No wonder he didn't approve when his disciples shooed the children away. Children are open, honest and uncluttered. They are not afraid to be themselves and are not afraid to want. The man at the pool could do with a child's heart and a child's response, but his desire has got lost somewhere along the way and his heart has become lost with it. It isn't irretrievable though. I like to think that before the man is healed, Jesus has stirred up a spark of desire within him. Can you imagine what looking into the eyes of Jesus is like?

How different this healing is from many others. In Matthew 9, for example, we find a woman who has suffered severe bleeding for twelve years. Because of her illness, she is ritually unclean and should not touch Jesus, but her desire is overwhelming. She knows what she has to do, and she wants to do it. Jesus heals her, and he commends her for her faith. And look at Hannah in 1 Samuel. Hannah is childless, but life is even worse for her because her husband has another wife, and this other wife has children and never stops rubbing it in. Year by year, and especially during their visits to the house of the Lord, Hannah becomes increasingly unhappy until one day she can bear it no longer and pours out her troubles to God. Thinking she is drunk, Eli the priest tells her off, but Hannah sets him straight. "I'm not drunk," she says, "I am desperate." Eli's tone changes immediately. "Go in peace," he says, "and may the God of Israel give you what you have asked him for." And the Lord answers her prayer with the boy Samuel, a key player in the history of the Israelite people. That's the result of so freely expressing her heart's desire.

In the Sermon on the Mount, Jesus doesn't hide the fact that he wants people to ask. He says it in three different ways, just in case we haven't got it the first time: "Ask, and you will receive; seek, and you will find; knock, and the door will be opened to you." [Matt.7:7] Don't be afraid to want, and don't be afraid to ask. It may go against everything that you have believed and everything that you have become, but it really is all right with God. Jesus says so.

THE DAY AFTER THE CLOCKS WENT BACK

Last night the clocks fell back, and at no cost
They handed me an extra sixty minutes
– One full hour with no agenda in it –
For me to use in ways that pleased me most;
And, in one twelfth the passing of the sun,
These are the things I could have done:
I could have spent the hour in prayer;
I could have washed my gardening wear.
I could have listened to a symphony by Brahms,
Or had a basking shark tattooed upon my arms.
I could have oiled my daughter's swing and set it straight,
Or scraped a decade's lichen from the gate.
I could have jumped, I could have skipped,
I could have sung, I could have whipped
A bowl of cream to have for lunch
Or tried to understand the credit crunch.
I could have written to an ancient uncle down in Putney;
I could have made some chutney, or some jam.
I could have sat crossed-legged on bean-bags
And had deep thoughts on who I am.
I could have telephoned my cousin Grace,
Or boiled three home-grown beetroot in a pan.
I could have sketched a likeness of my face,
Or spoken words of kindness to a dying man.
I suppose I could have planned the year ahead,
Or sent my application for the Great North Run;
Instead, I chose to spend another hour in bed,
And I thought of all the things I could have done.

A Prayer

Jesus,
I see this man by the pool,
And I think it isn't difficult
To fill his shoes.
I lose heart too, and with it hope,
And I've enough experience to know
That failure has the odds, and not success.
Wise to hold back, keep my imagination
Firmly in its box, like longing, and do my best
To be grown up about it. And yet
I see this isn't good enough for you.
Your eyes say that, your words the same:
"So, are you wanting to be well?"
I think I am. Somewhere inside
I am wanting, wanting to leap up, fearless,
Not tangled by this theatre, this audience,
This script I've learned
With someone else's lines.
So, ask me again, and I'll say yes,
And I will trust that power is yours
To give me freedom from myself,
And make me well.

31

No Limits

Numbers 11

YOU WOULD THINK THAT WITH A PILLAR OF FIRE OR A cloud either above them or going ahead of them, not to mention a good number of miraculous events behind them, the people of Israel would by now be walking in complete trust in their saving God. What we find, though, is exactly the opposite: each time an apparently insurmountable obstacle arises, the Israelites start complaining. Even Moses is not immune. The people complain that they don't have enough meat; Moses complains that he has too many people. The people say that they would rather be in Egypt; Moses says that he would rather be in the next life. There are problems everywhere, and nobody is ever happy.

I note two things here. The first is that we often complain to God about something, even claiming that this something is his fault, when we could go a long way towards solving the difficulty ourselves. Moses thinks he's in a hopeless situation: the responsibility for all these people is simply too much for him. "Just kill me now!" he cries, and he seems to mean it. But he's forgetting something, because when he was in a not dissimilar position in Exodus 18, his father-in-law rescued him with a very sound, common-sense proposal. At that time Moses was up from dawn till dusk settling disputes among the people. Jethro rightly pointed out that this was too much for one man and that Moses should appoint other judges to settle less weighty matters. So he did, and it worked. Much the same is going on here, and although Moses' frustration and anger may be understandable, he could use his experience of God and his experience of the past to help him approach both God and the people in a different way. In other words, he could ask for help. The fact that God has put Moses in a position of leadership doesn't, it turns out, mean that Moses has to do absolutely everything by himself. In fact it is essential that he doesn't. This can be a hard lesson to learn, not simply for leaders but for all of us. Jesus' desire that we love each other includes helping each other, and not simply offering help but also inviting the help that others are able and willing to give.

The second thing I notice is that the opposite of complaining isn't a stoical resignation to one's lot, the attitude that says, "We're stuck with it. There's nothing we can do, so we might as well grin and bear it." The opposite of complaining doesn't come close to that, because it involves looking to the Lord and it involves asking. Neither Moses nor the people understand this, but in verse 23 God sets them straight with words that we should repeat to ourselves several times a day: "Is there a limit to my power?" Our situation may be difficult and our complaining may be understandable, but this complaining is nothing less than a lack of trust, a failure to comprehend who God is, and therefore a failure to live in the relationship that he wants to have with us, that of father and child.

Asking does not come as easily as you might think. We grow up to believe that we should be self-sufficient, that we should stand on our own two feet, that there's nothing worse than being needy. It's a lie, of course, because our lives are continually showing us how difficult it is to remain in control, but still we find it hard to ask for help. Jesus does his best to encourage us. "Ask, and you will receive," he says. "For all those who ask will receive." [Lk.11:9-10] He says this in different ways on other occasions, encouraging us to open ourselves more and more to our Father's generous heart.

All of this means that because we ask less than we could, or should, our experience of God's generosity is more limited than it needs to be. It's a vicious circle. We don't ask and so we don't receive; we don't receive and so we don't develop the habit of faithfully asking. Isn't this why it's possible sometimes to experience answered prayer and be surprised that God has even heard us? Our natural response to God's "Is there a limit to my power?" is usually, "Yes there is: it's anything that concerns me." We need to learn otherwise, and we won't do that by complaining. Complaining is saying that everything starts and ends with me. The act of asking is the act of opening myself up to God's limitless possibilities.

One of the things we may hear as children is, "He who asks doesn't get," and in raising our own children we may well have told them something similar. That's why spending time with my grandchildren has been so helpful in this respect. Repeated requests from my own children produced in me something like irritation. When my grandchildren do the same, I find it charming and perfectly proper. One day when our eldest grand-daughters were quite small, we were bringing them home in the car from a day out, a journey of about an hour. Their granny had told them that once we had been travelling for a while, she would let each of them have a packet of Cheddars, their favourite. This was a mistake, of course, because to the girls "a while" meant "immediately", and Granny's subsequent "in ten minutes" meant "in ten seconds". In the end, and presumably in some sort of attempt to remain in control, Carol said, very calmly, "I will let you have them very soon, on condition that you don't mention the word Cheddars again." About half a minute passed, and then a little voice from the back piped up, "I'm not mentioning the word I'm not supposed to mention, but are we at 'very soon' yet?" And with this they got their Cheddars.

The saying "He who asks doesn't get" is not what Jesus says. He says the opposite. James says much the same in his letter: "You do not have what you want, because you do not ask God for it." Admittedly, he says that we should ask with the right motives, but he still encourages us to ask. Jesus says, "Ask, and go on asking." I suspect that we don't take this sufficiently seriously. I know I don't. I start well enough, perhaps, but the temptation to give up is quick to raise its head if the answers don't come rolling in more or less immediately. Why do I do that? Why don't I instead listen carefully to what Jesus is telling me and continue to ask, confident that our Lord hears and answers? Why do I dismiss Jesus' words so easily? Praying with a friend recently, we came to the end of a number of requests and sat for a moment in silence. Then my friend said, "I've heard Jesus thanking us for our prayers. He says he's passed them on to the Father." Not, we may assume, to be left in a pile of unread and unanswered mail.

So, is there an end to asking? Yes, and in the Garden of Gethsemane Jesus shows us that too. Faced with the ordeal he knows is coming, he asks to be spared. "Isn't there any other way?" he asks his Father. Then come the key words: "Yet not what I want, but what you want." [Matt.26:39] If the Lord makes it clear that his will is different from ours, then it is time to stop asking. For the Israelites in the desert, even the seemingly insurmountable problem of having no meat was not beyond God's limits. He simply diverted a large flock of migrating quail. But sometimes God may choose not to give us what we want because he wants something different or something better, and then our best response is still not to complain but simply to make a different request: "Lord, I ask only for what you want to give me."

182

HIS HANDS AND MINE

Fists clenched, I have claimed my independence,
My hard-won manhood, this battle-bruised right
To stand on these my own two feet, to fight,
To have, hold on to and experience
Such lordship in my doing; what prickles
Of pride run painful down my twisted spine,
Even as this long-lusted prize of mine
From in between my bleeding fingers trickles.
How differently does Jesus, cross-bound, live:
All unpossessing, hands turned out, unclasped,
Moment by moment open to receive
And joyfully pass on, not selfish grasp,
All that his heavenly Father has to give,
Much more even than he might think to ask.

A Prayer

Heavenly Father,
I take my prayer requests and list them,
Carefully and neatly, and in order of importance.
Then I consider them, carefully again,
And bring to you the ones I think are well expressed,
The ones you'll smile on most, are certain to agree with.
I try to keep emotion out of it. My job is done,
And you will do what you think best. A child
Works differently, lists prayer requests haphazardly,
Scribbles them, perhaps illegibly, gives importance
Not to one but all, each one as full of meaning
As the next, and then the child will rush them to you,
Assault you with them at a most unhelpful time,
Blurt out a couple more discovered in their headlong
Dash, eyes full of trust and expectation, knowing
That you love all this, and them, and that you will do
Everything you can to satisfy their longing. So,
Which would I be? It's not a hard decision, Lord:
I'll be the child. Come be my Father. Come help
Me off with this straitjacket I no longer want.
Come loosen my tongue. Come help me to pray.

32

Waiting for God

Psalm 37:1-11

LET'S FACE IT, NOBODY LIKES TO BE KEPT WAITING. LIFE'S short, and there aren't enough hours in the day to spend time hanging about. Fortunately for us, modern convenience comes to our rescue. For those in a headlong rush, more and more things are instant, not only tea and coffee but the whole meal if that's what you want. The other day, at a supermarket checkout, I stood next to a man who was buying seven identical ready meals. "That's me sorted for the next week," he said, with what seemed like a great sigh of relief. And if you don't want to queue, and if the quick and easy do-it-yourself aisle goes wrong for you every time as it does for me, then simply do it all from home. You shop, they drop. What could be better?

And it's not only food. Now you can watch just about anything *on demand*. Out of curiosity I googled this delightful little phrase and was amazed to see that it took no more than 0.26 seconds to come up with over one billion results. Just say the word, and you have more or less unlimited choice. Right now, in your home, on your settee. And if you can't afford something, put it on your credit card. Even better, find an offer that says, "Buy now, pay later." It doesn't matter that this really means, "Have now, buy later." Have it anyway, *because you're worth it!*

Good for me, I'm not guilty in some of these areas and find I'm not tempted to have the latest model to hit the market. I was made to have a mobile phone, because I once got lost and caused Carol a good deal of anxiety, but I haven't used it much and have to carry a list of instructions if I take it out with me. Our previous television was from the ark. When some friends came to dinner, the very first thing they said after hello was, "We have a spare set if you'd like it." Just to be polite, we said yes, but as the old television was still very much alive, it was some time before the pretender took its place. As for clothes, I possess one of the smallest wardrobes in the Western world. I just don't care.

But in other ways I'm no different at all, because there are situations in which I really don't like having to wait. I'm very bad, for example, at traffic lights, and I can't understand why some people have to drive so very slowly through them, sometimes pausing to ensure that nobody's coming from another direction. Telling myself that it's common practice in places like Italy, I sometimes toot my horn to try, invariably unsuccessfully, to speed people up, and I mutter silently, and not so silently, if I don't get through the lights the first time they're green. I'm the same with things that go wrong. If something needs fixing, I want it fixed now, no matter that our plumber, for example, isn't available until next week. My world is tipped off balance by such delays. When our bathroom was redone, I did experience a little of the adventurous spirit in having to go the sports centre for a shower, but I wouldn't have wanted to do it more than once.

I don't find waiting for God very easy either, so it's good that there's evidence in the Bible to suggest that we don't have to. "Let there be light," says God at the beginning of Genesis, "and light appeared." "Just give the order," says the Roman officer in Matthew 8, "and my servant will get well." And he does, at that very moment. It's true that occasionally Jesus' healings take a little longer. He spends time with a blind man, making mud and putting it on the man's eyes before the man can see clearly, but it seems fair to say that when Jesus gives the order, something happens, and people don't have to wait long. Usually there's no waiting involved at all, and that's how we like it.

But we know that this isn't the whole story, because other people, in other places and at other times, do a lot of waiting. Moses spent years as a shepherd before God appeared to him in the burning bush, and then another forty in the wilderness without ever arriving at the Promised Land. David was anointed king and then had to wait many years for the position to become vacant. Simeon and Anna spent a lifetime in prayer before their one revelation. Abraham and Sarah, and Elizabeth and Zechariah, had wanted a child for so long that when God said he was answering their prayer they simply didn't believe him. Mary and Martha had to face their brother's death, and Jairus his daughter's, before Jesus brought them back to life. So, if we feel we're having to wait for something, we're in good company.

"Be patient and wait for the Lord to act," writes David in Psalm 37. The trouble is, there's a bit of me that rebels against this. "Be patient" sounds like it's coming from an irritated parent to an irritating child, and I'm not an irritating child; I'm simply asking, and asking again, as Jesus encourages me to do. So I did what I often do at times like this; I looked up the psalm in my Spanish Bible, and I saw what I already knew but had somehow forgotten, that the Spanish for 'to wait' is the same as the Spanish for 'to hope' and 'to expect'. So when in English we read, "Wait patiently for the Lord", the Spanish reads, "Put your hope and trust in the Lord." How much better, I thought, than "I will wait patiently" is "I will wait with expectation, full of hope, trust and anticipation"? What might appear just a little negative, and for me a bit difficult, suddenly becomes positive and a good deal easier, like waiting for my summer holiday, only better.

Why be positive? Firstly, because, as David writes three Psalms later, "...he listened to me and heard my cry." [Ps.40:1] When we pray, God hears, even if we're tempted to believe that he doesn't, or can't, or won't listen *to us*. When the angel appears to Daniel three weeks after Daniel began praying, he says, "God has heard your prayers ever since the first day you decided to humble yourself in order to gain understanding." [Dan.10:12] "I have heard them cry out to be rescued," says God to Moses about the Israelites, "and so I have come down to rescue them from the Egyptians..." [Ex.3:7,8]

And there's the second thing: when we pray, God never does nothing. He may not answer as soon as you would like, but you won't be ignored. Just after Christmas last year I began to suffer from the sort of sciatic pain that my wife got to know only too well, not as bad as hers but still uncomfortable, so I went for prayer ministry one morning at church. Afterwards the pain was still there, as it was the next day and the day after that. In fact I settled back into it, and it was only about two weeks later that I realised that the pain had gone. God had answered my prayer and I hadn't even noticed!

Something even better happened just the other day. Within the space of half an hour I learned that two young women for whom I had been praying, both having or likely to have great difficulty in conceiving, were both expecting a child. One of these two had even fallen off the bottom of my prayer list. I had more or less forgotten her, but clearly God hadn't.

This waiting is also something to do with my maturing in the Lord. It's about patience in the best sense, about growing in anticipation and faith, about the transforming of my character and the increasing of my dependency on him. It is, as it always is, about relationship, a relationship with my heavenly Father and not with my heavenly Father Christmas. A friend told me about someone for whom he'd been praying for quite a time, and I asked him how he managed to keep on praying for the same thing over and over again. "I try to remember on each occasion that it doesn't depend on me," he said. "The Lord already knows, because I've told him, so all I have to do is lift it back up to him." The burden, it seemed, was being shouldered elsewhere. My friend could be still and he could wait hopefully. "And how long did you have to wait?" I asked. "About a year," he said, and his amused expression suggested that although this waiting had not been easy, it had been well worth it.

Such insights are not of much use to us unless we begin to practise their lessons in our daily life, and this I have attempted to do, at some times more successfully than at others. A good place to practise, I have found, is back in the supermarket queue where we started. As you've probably guessed, I'm not very good at queuing, so I am almost invariably given the opportunity to have yet another go at what I'll call "sanctified waiting". Very simply this means making a conscious effort not to be in any way stressed by a possible delay, and this might involve silently praying for and blessing both the checkout assistant and the person in front of me who wanted three bottles of ketchup, not two, and now has to go back for another one, or it might involve responding, eventually, to the poor assistant's apology with a cheerful, and increasingly genuine "Don't worry, I have all day," and then thanking them for their patience too. Such things can take the stress off me, and as an assistant once told me, it takes a little of the stress off them too. There are so many awkward customers, apparently, so let's try to be the exception, and let's bring great pleasure to our heavenly Father in the process, because these things do not go unnoticed.

CATHEDRAL

Space enough
To look outwards
And beyond;
Space enough
To look upwards
And wonder;
Space enough
To loiter
Hesitant
In shadows;
Space enough
To be painted
In bright colours
By sunlight
Falling
Silently
From high windows;
Space enough
To run fingers
Softly
Over stones
Soaked in prayer;
Space enough
To dance
Quietly
On the very edge of faith;
Space enough
To find one's own space
And calmly exhale.

A Prayer

Father,
I wait, not easily
But fretfully, impatiently.
I ask, not always trusting
That you've heard me, and
Very often not prepared
To leave my prayers with you, for you
To answer in your time.
Help me, Father, to wait, with hope
And joyful expectation.
Help me to be still in my waiting,
And know that as I wait
You will renew my strength.
You will let me soar like eagles,
Run and not grow weary,
Walk and not faint.

33

The Tortoise and the Hare

Philippians 3:1-14

IN MY PRESENT CHURCH FAMILY THERE ARE MANY WHO regularly receive pictures from God, usually in the setting of prayer, and these pictures are shared with the church or the smaller group present at the time or with an individual being prayed for, whichever is appropriate. Sometimes these pictures are uplifting and bring encouragement; sometimes they foretell events. They are always a powerful sign that God is involved in our lives, very often when we might have thought that he wasn't.

A friend of mine has exercised this gift since a powerful experience of the Holy Spirit some years ago, and I have been privileged to receive a few of these pictures. What I have found is that they are usually unpredictable; they are unexpected, often visually arresting, and can make you hold your breath for a moment. They are also personally relevant. I say to myself, "This cannot be made up; this really is for me."

After a significant step forward in my spiritual life about eight years ago, I fell into what I perceived to be a time of getting nowhere. It was disappointing and frustrating. Why had God taken me forward simply to leave me adrift? I shared this with my friend, and we prayed together about it. Then she gave me a picture that she had received from God for me. I still smile when I think about it, and it still encourages. In the picture was a long row of tortoises, all lined up at the start of a race. And she had received these words: "Don't rush. Don't strive. You will finish the race, and the prize will be yours."

Here's the first thing: God's pace is the only pace. We are to keep pace with him, not the other way round. We can rush ahead – most of us try to at some stage, and some of us never stop – but as in Aesop's fable, the rushing hare was beaten by the tortoise after the hare had fallen asleep, and he hadn't fallen asleep because he was tired but because he was doing things in his own way. The truth is that he didn't attach much importance to the race, and of course he had his incredible speed to fall back on, so why not take a nap by the roadside? However contradictory it may seem, if I am a hare I risk falling by the wayside, whereas if I care about the race I'll be a tortoise.

So we are all tortoises. I think it's significant that despite the connection between my friend's picture and Aesop's fable, there are no hares in this picture, just tortoises. We all look the same. We are all on the same starting line. We are all invited to travel at a tortoise's pace. There's no point in trying to psych out the opposition two minutes before the starting gun by asking, "What's your personal best?" They're just tortoises, and so am I. We're all going to be slow.

Unfortunately for tortoises, they look rather stupid. Maybe, just maybe, there's a certain wisdom in their faces, but on the whole they look a bit thick and very old, even when they're young. If you had to be an animal, nobody in the world would choose to be a tortoise. You'd have to have real humility. But here's the amazing part: you will finish the race and you will win the prize. Go at God's pace and you will get there, however slowly you may think you are going, however little progress you may think you are making. When I first received this picture, I thought, "How wonderful! I'm going to beat the rest of them. I wonder what my prize will be." (Pride comes even after being turned into a tortoise.) But then I realised, with a little disappointment, that if we are all tortoises, and if we all travel at God's pace, then we will all win the prize. The prize, after all, isn't simply a medal that we'll put in a drawer and forget about. It's something much bigger and much better than that, something that the Lord himself, infinitely more than we ourselves, is working towards: "And so I am sure that God, who began this good work in you, will carry it on until it is finished on the Day of Christ Jesus." [Phil.1:6]

And now here are two things that make this picture wonderfully relevant to me. Firstly, I have always enjoyed running. Even in my sixties, I still compete; badly, and with an increasing lack of success, but I still do it. So the irony isn't lost on me. God is telling somebody who likes to run fast – or fastish – that he has to run more slowly. I see the humour in it, but it's not easy.

Secondly, my friend was not previously aware of the close link between this picture and the verse given to me at my baptism nearly forty years before: "So I run straight towards the goal in order to win the prize, which is God's call through Christ Jesus to the life above." [Phil.3:14] It's Paul's picture of an athlete in a race, setting his sights on the finishing line, focusing his mind on the prize to be won. I have discovered that life is full of things that will try to distract us from doing that, not least our willingness to believe that it's all going so very slowly. It's as well to remember that if you see an athlete running a race with tightened muscles in his limbs and pain on his face, he is unlikely to win. He's trying too hard; he isn't at ease with himself or with the race. We can only win in the grace and at the pace that God gives us, because, as in Ecclesiastes 9:11, "fast runners do not always win the race". It is, after all, a race for tortoises, even for tortoises like St Paul, who was clearly glad to have been running in it.

"I have done my best in the race, I have run the full distance, and I have kept the faith. And now there is waiting for me the victory prize of being put right with God, which the Lord, the righteous Judge, will give me on that Day – and not only to me, but to all those who wait with love for him to appear." [2.Tim.4:7-8]

IN SINGING SILENCE

I wish that it were possible to catch
That unexpected magic moment when
I turn the corner of another street,
Walking weary in my workday feet,
And see against an unforgiving sky
A rainbow, or the faintest hint of one,
That for a second beckons, and is gone.

I would give so much to have again
Those hours that followed on from our first landing
In Mallorca: thick, warm butter blackness
Of that foreign air; the moped madness;
Soft scents of pine and oleander;
And everywhere the song of nightingales
Pinned new horizons back with liquid nails.

And how I wish that I could parcel up
And keep preserved like orange marmalade
The unspoilt joy of childhood Christmases:
Decorations only half remembered; promises
Of presents merely guessed at, worth more
To me than all their weight in chocolate gold;
The sense that something extraordinary might unfold.

Thus is my worship. My words fall always
Short of adoration, and my body,
Stiff and suited, bends with such resistance
It were made of stone. But then, in singing silence,
Hidden in the hollow of the mountain rock,
I see my Lord pass by, for just one moment even,
And I am caught, like rainbows, there between earth and heaven.

A PRAYER

Lord, I'm just a tortoise,
And so I ask you for your grace,
When I compare myself to faster runners,
To remember that you are my creator,
And that I am fearfully and wonderfully made.

Lord, I'm just a tortoise,
And so I ask you for your grace,
When I think how slow I must be going,
To remember I must walk as Jesus walked:
Justly, lovingly, in humble fellowship with you.

Lord, I'm just a tortoise,
And so I ask you for your grace,
When I see other athletes rushing past,
To remember that you guide me on good paths
And make me rest by quiet streams.

Lord, I'm just a tortoise,
And so I ask you for your grace,
When I am tempted to wander off the track,
To remember that the path to life is narrow,
But that you have promised to walk it by my side.

Lord, I'm just a tortoise,
And so I ask you for your grace,
When I come close to losing heart,
To remember that your desire is my good finishing,
And that you urge me on, on towards my promised prize
In Jesus, creator and finisher of this race.

34

Learning a New Language

Acts 10

I HAVE DONE A LITTLE PRIVATE TUITION RECENTLY, AND I have been reminded of something which has always surprised me, and this is the almost fierce resistance that many pupils show towards learning a foreign language. The fact is that while we show resistance, progress is slower than it needs to be. When learning a new language, we are often reluctant to accept that things are done differently. We baulk at rules; we baulk when rules are broken. Why can't they just speak English like we do? We feel that we are in control of our own language, and we wish, perhaps unconsciously, to be in control when we're learning somebody else's. Why can't they do it our way?

And yet it's only by submitting ourselves to the language that we can begin to master it. Or, more accurately, we become increasingly free in the new language when we begin to let it master us, when we don't argue with it, fight it, try to change it, but instead open ourselves up to it, to its new ways of doing things, its idiosyncrasies and even its perceived absurdities. When we let it wash over us, fill us, even delight us, then and only then do we begin to experience freedom in it. Put simply, I express myself most freely in the new language when I learn to let the new language express itself most freely in me.

My experience is that this is equally true of the life of the Spirit, though here too it is seldom an easy lesson to learn. You only have to look at Peter in Acts 10. The Spirit of God was in the process of reaching out to the Gentiles, but the believers, even the apostles, had come nowhere near to catching up. One suspects from this chapter that Peter would not have expected, and would not have wanted, God to include the Gentiles in his plan of salvation. Why would God do that? The Jews were a people kept apart for God. God was therefore a God kept apart for the Jews. Except that he wasn't, and even before Peter had his vision, Cornelius, a Gentile, was having one of his own.

Peter's vision comes with a message repeated three times, and still Peter doesn't know what it means. He has to be led. Cornelius' men have to arrive, the Spirit has to urge Peter to go with them, Peter has to hear about Cornelius' vision, and he has to witness with his own eyes the falling of the Spirit on this Gentile family. Even then Peter's companions, and maybe Peter too, are amazed. All credit to them, because they accept what the Spirit is teaching them, but they are amazed nonetheless. You can sense Peter's surprise in the next chapter, when he tells the believers in Jerusalem that "when I began to speak, the Holy Spirit came down on them". It's when he *begins* to speak. God doesn't even wait for Peter to get half way through his sermon, something I wish had happened during many of the sermons I have found myself listening to over the years.

Although Peter is learning a new language, the language of the Spirit, he isn't as open to the Spirit's way of doing things as he thinks he is. Even after Pentecost, when the Spirit comes in power, Peter is still looking at things through the eyes of his religion, and one has a sense that in too many ways his religion and his God are close to being the same thing. God shows him that they aren't. Jesus has spent three years showing him that they aren't, but a new language is difficult to learn. We bring to it old formulae and old frameworks, and whilst these appeared to work well before, they are of no real use to us now. Jesus says that the Spirit will teach us all things, but the Spirit also has to help us unlearn a great many things, some of which we might have thought important enough to build our life on and which we don't give up without a fight. And this is a fundamental part of his religion that Peter has to give up, so by extension there exists the possibility, always, that as the Spirit moves us forward he will show us aspects not only of our life in general but specifically of our religion that he will urge us to relinquish. Maybe because these things were simply a step up to get us going or a crutch that we no longer need. Maybe because they are now proving unhelpful, or simply because they are untrue. In the end it will be because we are continuing to impose our own rules on the new language. We are making God in our own image. We don't think we are, because it's our religion, and we're doing it religiously, even if we have read the parable of the prodigal son a thousand times. There's always an interesting moment at the beginning of an A level language course when you let pupils know that the framework they have been building on for the past few years is less firm than they thought it was. It was not necessarily untrue; rather, it was incomplete and needed to be reworked and expanded. There are always groans, but if the pupils mean business they soon get over it. They have to.

As a language teacher I have invariably been a bit touchy (touchy, but calm and controlled, naturally) when people have said to me, in a rather superior tone that always irritates, "Of course, the best way to learn a language is to go and live in the foreign country." There's a large degree of truth in that, I'll grant you, but: one, you know they've never done it themselves and probably can't get past 'Bonjour'; two, thousands of British expats prove that as a generalisation it's rubbish; and three, the best way to learn a new language is to be a little child. Jesus has told us that, probably several times, but we just don't listen.

Carol and I scattered the ashes of three of our parents. They were moving events, as you might imagine, although a certain lightness, and even humour, were added by a strong wind which blew on each occasion and which ensured even more of a scattering than we had intended.

A SCATTERING

Dead now
Dust and ashes
Ashes and dust
White sand-cupped hands
Life wind-borne
Hawthorn silver painted
For Christmas
Homeward trail along the path

Gone now
The roots
The tree to lean against
The sounding board
The point of reference
The affirming smile
The reflected self

Not now
The weekly call
The outer wall
The safety net
The open door
The living photographs
The borrowed space

But now
Another call
A knowing all
Even as we are known
Hands without blotches
Eyes without secrets
No switching on the dark

But light, always light
And future

A PRAYER

Heavenly Father,
Let me not shelter
From the wind of your Spirit.
Let me, instead, stand
Out in it, on a hill even,
Enjoy it, risk being blown away!

Heavenly Father,
Let me not fear
The river of your Spirit.
Let me, instead, dip
My toes in it, my feet,
Swim in it, risk being swept away!

Heavenly Father,
Let me not hide
From the freedom of your Spirit.
Let me, instead, climb
Down from my own picture,
Walk, run, risk being brought to life!

35

Grumpy Old Men

Luke 1:5-23,57-66

TODAY MOST PEOPLE WOULD PROBABLY SAY THAT CHRIST-
mas is a time for children, *the* time for children, and just about
everything about our modern Western Christmases suggests that
they're right. Toy adverts on television begin in early autumn, the role
of presents has assumed overwhelming proportions, parties come thick
and fast, and most recently and in the absence of the real thing, houses
and gardens are adorned to overflowing with Santas, snowmen,
reindeer and an incalculable number of light bulbs. It's possible to see
the winter wonderland in your neighbour's garden. Maybe even in
yours. It's magic.

As for adults, that's a different matter. True, there are some who
have managed to retain their childlike heart, but for many the magic
has well and truly worn off. They may try to recapture it at the office
party or by watching Mary Poppins, but these things seldom work. You
can't try to capture a sense of the magical; it just happens. A lot of us
simply bypass the whole occasion, a part of us glad that we have,
another part feeling a regret that we can't quite explain. Almost
inevitably we end up feeling grumpy. I know I do.

A year or two ago we watched a programme entitled *Grumpy Old
Men at Christmas*. Carol said I could have co-written the script. That's
not quite true, because I could have written the whole thing by myself.
And I'm not going to feel too guilty here, because I think there's an
awful lot to be grumpy about. I try to console myself with the thought
that Christmas isn't really a time for adults, but I'm wrong because
adults are precisely the people Christmas is for. Take a look at the
biblical narratives. With the exception of Jesus and John, the other key
players are all adults, and some of them are getting on a bit. Jesus and
John are gifts at Christmas, gifts coming to adults who are in some
cases ready to receive and in others not quite so ready; in some cases
not ready at all, in others positively against it.

Surprise, surprise: those most ready were the oldest and definitely not the grumpiest, Simeon and Anna. How long had the Messiah been promised? For centuries, yet here they were on the edge of their seats, praying, fasting and very ready for God to break into their lives. For them, God's intervention was always possible in the now, so they weren't surprised when it happened. They had left time and place to God, but they lived tuned in to a God who didn't break his promises.

We might have expected Zechariah to be the same, but he wasn't. As the priests took it in turns to burn the incense, this may have been the only occasion on which Zechariah did it. A good man, upright and God-fearing, he was undertaking his priestly duty in accordance with Mosaic institution, and perhaps this was the biggest day of his life. Zechariah was the special one, the representative of Man before God, a man set aside in the holy place, and if ever something extraordinary was going to happen, today would be the day. And it did, and it was, and Zechariah wasn't having any of it.

When an army moves forward it repeatedly consolidates its position. Unless prearranged, it's important not to have units out on a limb, but when the Spirit of God moves people forward, they invariably find themselves out on a limb. When you're dealing with the Spirit of God, this is the best place to be. It's not the safest, but it is the best. To look at the church, you wouldn't think so, because we do all that we can, consciously or not, to consolidate positions. Hence form and structure, rules and systems, not necessarily wrong in themselves, but capable of supplanting the onward, unpredictable movement of God's Spirit. So it is that we can attend church faithfully and perform all our duties correctly, under the impression, even if not formulated in so many words, that we have arrived. Is this where Zechariah was on that day? Had he arrived?

Over the years I have been bad in this respect. I have often confused the church which belongs to God with the God who owns the church. And here I mean church in the wrong sense: the organisation, not the people. I think if I had focused more on the people, I would have been closer to the heart of God, but that hasn't usually been the case. I have been to more meetings than I would have liked where we concentrated almost entirely on little more than keeping the church ticking over, usually meaning in the same way as before. I don't remember us ever talking about how the engine could be turbo-charged.

Surely, such a bias is inappropriate in a people who profess a dynamic, life-changing and presumably church-changing God, but it's easy to get this wrong. We can take refuge, even pleasure and pride, in form and structure, and bit by bit the God for whom we're doing it becomes increasingly indistinct until he fades from view like the Cheshire Cat. At the beginning of each service we usually welcome newcomers and are in the habit of welcoming God too, but we might be alarmed if the God who turns up this week does so in a rather different way from the manner in which he turned up last week, that quiet way which meant that we didn't actually notice him.

Perhaps I'm being hard on Zechariah. It could be that whilst he was doing everything he should as priest and man (he was, after all, commended by God for his righteousness), his God simply wasn't big enough. During the many years of his honest and dutiful religion, Zechariah may have come to believe that what he had was, for him at least and in this life at least, all there was to have. It's easy to feel like this. How many of us, for example, see angels even once in a lifetime or experience a miracle? How many of us expect our spiritual experience this week to be any different from last week's, or to be any different in a year's time? The truth is that I have met people whose relationship with God has been unchanged for most of their lives. Great chunks of my own life have been the same. We may be upright in our conduct, regular in our attendance and dutiful in our service, but there is about us a certain resignation: this is the way it is. And we get used to it. In time we take comfort from it. We may even come to prefer it that way.

In Zechariah's case this resignation was linked to the child that he and his wife didn't have. Don't you think they had prayed to their God time and time again? Their God was a faithful and generous God. Their God had answered the prayers of women like Hannah who knew the ache in the heart of the childless. It went without saying then that God would answer their prayer too, but he hadn't. And the years passed, and bit by bit it must have seemed to them that God was denying their request, and what could they do about it? How could they fight the will of God? Their prayers were bouncing off a heaven as hard as brass, and they would just have to get used to it. For the most part, and especially Zechariah, I suspect they did.

But God hadn't ignored their prayer, he simply wasn't ready to answer it. He wasn't denying them a child; he was going to give them a very special child who could not have been born when the time wasn't right. This couple couldn't have understood so many years before that the time wasn't right for them, but now their lives were about to be

204

turned upside down. Look again at the angel's first words: "Don't be afraid, Zechariah! God has heard your prayer..."

And here's another problem for poor Zechariah. Not only was he not expecting an angel to visit him, not only was he not expecting God to intrude upon his religious service, he wasn't expecting to be fathering a child at his age. It was nice of God to get around to answering his prayer, but wasn't God aware of how things actually worked? I love this bit of the story. I love the way in which the angel details not only the child's birth but also the extraordinary facts about the life to follow. This boy isn't going to be your average child. He will be like Elijah; he will usher in the Lord himself. There won't have been a child like him. Was this an answer to prayer or what? Good news upon good news. Even for the angel it's almost unbelievable.

Faith, they say, believes when it cannot see. It obeys when it doesn't understand. It goes ahead, not knowing the road. It gives thanks even if it hasn't yet received. Is that where you are with your prayers? When God answers your prayers, will he catch you out like he did Zechariah, who had to be taught a lesson and silenced for a while? When God answers your prayers, will he find you alongside him? "Let's get going," says God. "But how?" we say, and God isn't amused. We've failed the test. Zechariah, though, comes through with a little help from the Lord. When the baby is born, everybody wants to name him after his dad. That was the proper thing to do. *Not a chance,* thinks the silent Zechariah. *I've learned my lesson. His name is John, a gift from God.* Quite right. God is back where he belongs, and so is Zechariah.

NATIVITY

As if frozen in time,
The players in this annual Nativity
Assume the place to each assigned
By custom and tradition,
Take their habitual position
In this now perfected composition.
While plaster faces smile, adore,
The animals attend on unsoiled straw
In just the way that they stood last year
And the years before.

But we move on, and I feel no longer
That strange stirring in the boy-child that I was.
With age I notice chapped lips, a chipped finger,
Colour fading from their eyes, these men and women
Slipping away even as I look at them, as if weary
Of all the weight of story we have placed on them,
Their attitude interpreted, imposed, by scholars, clergy,
Passers-by who for a moment pause,
And children who have mixed them up with Santa Claus.
Should I be sad? Better, perhaps, to understand
A different message from these characters:
Not graven images, but servants too, like angels,
Who gently step aside, refuse to take his place,
And crack and crumble even as I watch, even as
This cosy scene is decked with fairy lights and holly,
Even as the flashing Christmas tree insists that we be jolly.

Not jolly, surely, for the first Christmas was a very dark affair.
No room in the place where people stay,
No welcome, nothing much beyond the vacant stare
That says you don't belong and never will;
Foreign, if you like, alien, turned away
With the chills running through you:
Chill of the deepening shadows,
Chill of the cold, unfamiliar streets,
Chill of the awful uncertainty of it all,

An uncertain past, an uncertain future,
And an imminent, uncertain birth,
The shadow of death hanging like a curtain
Around the little town, the devil sitting by a log fire
Waiting for opportunities, and faith, or something like faith,
Hanging by a single thread from a low branch.

But then there was light,
Or, at the very least, there was light enough.
Light enough for wise men to see where they were going,
For the sick to find their way to the healer;
Light enough for the pure in heart to see God,
For the sorrowful to know comfort,
For the merciful to receive mercy.
Light enough, in fact, to set the night sky ablaze,
Put fear and fire into the eyes of shepherds,
Cause them to act quite out of character
And tumble like snowmelt down over low hills,
Seized by something for which
They would never have the right words,
Something they caught, momentarily, in each other's eyes
As they stood around, awkwardly, these
Sons of the morning, to whom
Had been given, like a precious gift,
This new thing that had moved inside them:
Something longed for, but given up on,
Something that was never going to happen,
Something like the first kick of a child in an empty womb.

A Prayer

Lord God,
May I have the courage, should an angel
One day stand in front of me,
Not to run away and hide.

Lord God,
May I have the wisdom, should an angel
One day bring your word to me,
To lend both ears to it.

Lord God,
May I have the willingness, should an angel
One day voice your call to me,
To say, "Yes, Lord. Here I am, send me."

36

The Meaning of Words

Jeremiah 36

I LOVE WORDS. THEY WERE MY JOB FOR MORE THAN twenty-five years, and my fascination with them hasn't diminished. I love the sound of words, their form, and how they can be put together to create shades of meaning. I like word games and puzzles, wordplay and wit. In church it's a pleasure for me to listen to the Bible reading. Most people want to find the passage in their own copy, even though they miss the first few verses while they look for it, scratching around like a hornet in a paper bag. Not me. I want to listen. I want the words to smack me in the face.

Not everybody loves words. Some people hate them and would be happier if they didn't exist. Most people learn to speak their own language, but foreign languages can be an impossibility. Spelling is a headache for many and a nightmare for some. Reading can be slow and the understanding of it difficult. Some have linguistic flair; many more have a linguistic block. Some people are built not to be very much at home with words, so you shouldn't worry if that's you. If you like, it's God's fault.

There are a lot of words in the Bible, but they aren't simply words on a page in the sense that the words of a novel are. The words are telling a story, certainly, but it's the story of God's relationship with his people. Where does God begin speaking? In verse three of Genesis. Where in the Bible does God stop speaking? At the end of Revelation. From the beginning to the end, God is speaking. He is giving his word to his people.

Words depend on and reflect the nature of the person who says them. Each of us wants to hear the words "I love you", but these precious words only have real meaning if they mirror a truth in the speaker. Even these three beautiful words can be used to manipulate and control. In themselves words are empty vessels, their life depending on the life of the speaker. It follows that the words which God speaks are dependable, because God himself is dependable. This is made clear in the creation story. God speaks and it happens, and it happens in the exact way and to the exact extent that God said it, neither more nor less.

I wish it were as simple for us. Instead, when hearing God's "I love you", we may respond not with faith and hope but with suspicion and fear. In the ups and downs of life we learn to be suspicious of others, even to mistrust them, and we treat God in the same way. Then God speaks, and though what he says must happen, we're not so sure. We dither and make excuses. The word of God is daylight at the end of a tunnel, but we won't see it. We prefer to look behind us into the darkness; at least we know the way we've come.

It seems to be in the nature of man to respond to God in this way. God tells Abraham that he will father a great nation, but Abraham doesn't believe him. Instead he prefers to sort things out for himself, and he does it badly. Moses is told that he will be used to free the Israelites from slavery, but Moses doesn't believe God either. "I am nobody," says Moses. "How can I go...?" "Because of who I am," says God. "Because of who I have been and will be. Because I am the one true and faithful God, and because when I speak, it happens." But still Moses says, "No, Lord, don't send me."

Of course, Abraham became the father of a great nation, just as God had predicted, and Moses led the Israelites out of Egypt. They may not have believed, but it happened just as God had said, and so with such great examples of God's word in action you would think that his people would then attach great importance to it and be quick to respond in the way that he intended. Sadly not; the history of God's people is a story of his word more unobserved than observed, very often disobeyed, and sometimes even trampled underfoot. But God did not give up. From time to time he raised up those who spoke boldly the message he had given them. Sometimes the Israelites heeded the message, but all too often they continued in sin and disobedience, treating the word of God with contempt. King Jehoiakim, in Jeremiah 36, uses the word of God for nothing more than keeping his winter fire going!

"Words, words, words...!" complains Eliza Doolittle in her desire for something more. In the end God too knew, as he had always known, that something more would be required. The history of the Israelites had shown that God's love for them was undying, but it had also shown that his word to them had all too often fallen on deaf ears. A word was still needed, but a different sort of word. People needed a word that could not be ignored or misunderstood, a word that one could not just hear, but see and touch and experience: a living word. And so, "The word became a human being and, full of grace and truth, lived among us." [Jn.1:14]

Words may be empty vessels, but not this one, for "the full content of divine nature lives in Christ, in his humanity". [Col.2:9] This is all the fullness. Everything that God is, Jesus is. This word is overflowing with meaning and is vibrant with the life of the living God: "Whoever has seen me has seen the Father." [Jn.14:9] On the Mount of Transfiguration God says, "This is my own dear Son – listen to him!" [Mk.9:7] There can be no mistaking the message now. Or so you would think.

Jesus knows better. He tells us about himself in the parable of the tenants in the vineyard. The implication is clear: in the present age this word of God, this word made flesh, will not have a better reception among some than God's word ever had. "But when the tenants saw the son, they said to themselves, 'This is the owner's son. Come on, let's kill him, and we will get his property!' So ... they killed him." [Matt.21:38]

So it's just as well that God's punctuation, like his use of words, has much more life than ours. Punctuation can leave us in as much of a muddle as spelling, but we're usually safe with a full stop. We like what the full stop represents: a clear, crisp finality, a sense of loose ends tied up, even if the outcome isn't quite what we'd expected or even wanted. If necessary, a full stop lets us cut our losses; it allows us to abandon the project we've started and begin again.

But God does things differently, because he is nowhere near as keen on full stops as we are, preferring instead commas followed by 'and' or 'but'. Our judging others, our unbelief, our lack of faith, our giving up hope, these are all full stops, and with them we say, "That's it. There's nothing beyond this point." Zacchaeus was a full stop until he met Jesus, as were Matthew and Mary Magdalene. I was a full stop and so were you. Jesus' death was a full stop, or so everybody thought. In fact, it was simply a comma followed by 'and' or 'but': "The light shines in the darkness, and the darkness has never put it out." [Jn.1:5] What we thought was the end was in fact only the beginning. So you mustn't worry if you're not very good at using words or punctuation. Instead just be very glad that God is an expert at it.

CHRISTMAS

Throw together every icon of that Christmas,
Heap them up: the wandering shepherds wondering
About a child; an innkeeper blundering
His fifteen famous minutes; a sky filled
With angels and a shining star; three wise men,
Or more, arriving at an unexpected door;
Gifts wrapped in meaning; little Bethlehem; and then
Consider how much more meaningful than each of these,
At first a nothing, like the smell of ox and ass,
Those words of introduction: And it came to pass...

A PRAYER

Lord,
I thank you that you are not a God of endings
But of new beginnings. I thank you that your purposes
For me, and for the world, are good, that what you do
Is so much better than what I do, that your thoughts
Are so much more beautiful than mine, and that you chose
Not to lift Jesus down from the cross
But, instead, to raise him from the dead.
And so I choose to believe that what you have begun in me,
And in the world, you will bring to glorious completion,
And I am convinced that nothing in heaven or earth
Can separate me from your love, revealed to me so perfectly
In the death and resurrection of my Saviour, Jesus.

37

Lifting Up Our Eyes

2 Chronicles 32:1-23; 2 Kings 19:8-19

I DON'T KNOW HOW LONG YOUR PRAYER LIST IS, BUT MINE can seem pretty long sometimes. A couple of weeks ago, during a quiet time on a Saturday morning and praying again for people who had been on my list for quite a while, I felt that the load was becoming a little heavy, and I asked God how I could best continue to pray for them. The words that came into my mind almost straight away were, "Lift up your eyes."

I let these words sit with me for a while. They made sense, but I'm conscious that we can fool ourselves even more easily than we can fool others, so I asked God to confirm these words if indeed they were from him. The following morning the message at church was the second in a series on the Fruit of the Spirit, and this week it was about joy. "How could any of us," asked our vicar, "experience joy when we're in the middle of difficult circumstances?" Answer in a nutshell: by lifting up our eyes.

So, if there is a word here for me, it would seem to be that when praying, I'm not always looking in the right direction. If I'm honest that's probably true, and especially with my prayer list. Here are people I have prayed for very often, and when answers to prayer come with apparent slowness – or not at all – I do experience a growing lack of confidence, even of mild despair. My eyes, together with the rest of me, become downcast. I pray, but perhaps I am increasingly not expecting anything to happen. I'm not so much lifting my eyes to God as lowering them to myself. I'm bringing my burden to Jesus because he has offered to take its weight from me, but then I'm picking it up again and continuing to carry it as if nothing has happened. I'm forgetting that although Jesus said, "Pick up your mat and walk," he didn't say, "Pick up your burden and walk."

It was at this time that I was reading about King Hezekiah, and I saw interesting parallels here too. The accounts in 2 Kings 18-20 and 2 Chronicles 32 are different in terms of both detail and point of view, but what spoke to me is common to both. Unlike very many of the kings of the time, Hezekiah "did what was pleasing to the Lord". It wasn't simply that he was a God-fearing man; it was also because he set the nation back on the right track by doing away with pagan worship and by reforming religious life. And "he was successful, because everything he did for the Temple or in observance of the Law, he did in a spirit of complete loyalty and devotion to his God". So nothing could possibly have gone wrong.

But it did, because the Assyrians were on the warpath; they were invading Judah and coming to the very walls of Jerusalem. Hezekiah responds in a number of ways. In 2 Kings we see him acceding to the Assyrians' demands by handing over large quantities of treasure and hoping they'll go away – but they don't. So Hezekiah reinforces and re-equips his troops, and succeeds in cutting off the enemy's water supply. To his credit, he also assembles his soldiers and gives great encouragement by reminding them that because God is on their side they have considerably more power than the enemy does. But then the Assyrians play their trump card. They tell the Judaeans that this simply isn't true, that Hezekiah's God is no different from the hand-fashioned gods of those nations they have trampled underfoot. They tell them that God won't save them, because, to put it simply, he can't. Because he isn't God, in fact.

And what is Hezekiah's response? He lifts his eyes to the Lord. All right, so he's still concerned about himself and his people. But he's also concerned – more concerned, I think – about who his God is and about the way in which his God has been insulted. He's asking to be rescued – of course he is – but over and above this he desires the honour and the good name of his God. He asks to be rescued "so that all the nations of the world will know that only you, O Lord, are God".

I think I frequently miss this when I pray. All too often I forget that when Jesus taught his disciples to pray he taught them to start with, "Our Father in heaven: May your holy name be honoured." I might sometimes tack this on to the end of my prayers, but more often than not I leave it out altogether. What Hezekiah's prayer seems to be telling me is that I've got the whole thing upside down. I focus on the problem and then I ask God to help. Hezekiah focuses on God and only then does he ask for help, and this not principally for his own sake but for God's. When I pray for people, I need to ask myself if I am principally concerned – or even a little bit concerned – that God should be honoured and glorified in their lives. Or do I go straight to what I think is the heart of the matter, the problem to be solved, and never get beyond it?

In the story of Hezekiah – as always, I suppose – God has the last word. After the angel of the Lord has killed the Assyrian army, the emperor Sennacherib returns home in disgrace, only to be killed by two of his sons in the temple of his god, a place where, if anywhere, his god should have been able to save him. But he doesn't, because he can't. Because he isn't God, in fact.

HALO

APRIL 2020

Wuhan, a city once blissfully unknown
To most, will now be,
Like Chernobyl,
For ever quarantined
In the lockdown of our memory.

Several steps ahead of men and women
Dressed in white suits and empty streets,
This fresh disease, seeded
In fevers and in rasping coughs,
Has seen itself go viral.

We are each one affected, and with fear
Or pain or morbid curiosity we hear
Announced each afternoon the loss
Of hundreds more, and then, in *staying home*,
Of prepositions once considered permanent.

They say we are at war, and
As in war, we see a sharpening
Of who we are. The anxious fret,
The hoarders hoard, the critics
Carp at every opportunity, and yet

Hearts show through the cracks in our skin,
Impelling us to volunteer, applaud,
To melt before an old man pacing each one
Of his remaining days, to step courteously
Aside, exchanging non-infectious smiles.

And there are those who pray, who walk
Each day the tightrope of their faith, offer in their
Outstretched hands a world too big to hold,
And speak the old, unchanging words:
Lord, have mercy. Christ, have mercy. Lord, have mercy.

A PRAYER

Come, Holy Spirit,
And bring to me the peace of Jesus that he promises.
And how much I need it now,
When bad news shrieks from every screen;
When men and women wander hopeless,
And children, robbed of childhood, wonder;
When energy is sapped by dread
Of missiles and contagion, by fears
For loss of family, of friends, of work
And framework, and by numbness
At this shaking of the nations,
At this earth that either burns or drowns.
Come, Holy Spirit,
Share my Lord's untroubled heart with me,
And let my troubled thoughts be stayed on him,
That I might know his love, and rest in perfect peace.

38

Looking Up Again

2 Kings 6:8-23; Luke 8:40-56

LIFTING UP OUR EYES DOESN'T COME NATURALLY TO US. For one thing it's potentially dangerous, because we might bump into things. Now factor in that dizzy sensation you feel when you look up at shifting clouds, when you wonder whether it really is the clouds that are moving and not you. Talking about Paris with my godson, I once asked him if, unlike me, he would happily go up the Eiffel Tower. "I'd go up it," he said, "but I wouldn't be able to stand on the ground and look up at it."

More importantly, looking up is not what we're used to doing, because there are too many interesting things going on around us. Our youngest daughter once went to Salisbury for the weekend. Before she left I advised her to have a look at the cathedral, because I thought she'd be impressed. On her return I quizzed her. "So, did you go into the city?" "Yes, we did," she said. "And what did you make of the cathedral?" "I didn't see it," she replied. "But it has the tallest spire in England!" I spluttered. "It may have," she said, "but I didn't look up."

Elisha's servant in 2 Kings 6 didn't look up either, at least not at first. At first what he did was to look straight ahead, and after that he looked all around him. No matter where he looked, there were Syrian soldiers, and the Syrian soldiers were looking right back at him. And what you see is what you get. Of all our senses, our sense of sight is probably the one we rely on most. We know that a conjuror's trick is an illusion, and we know, often despite our instincts, that the camera can in fact lie, but on the whole we know that if we can see something, we can be as certain as we need to be that this something is there. If we can see it, it's real, and if it's real and dangerous then it's the only reality that matters, which is why Elisha's servant is terrified.

"We are doomed," he exclaims. And this is why we too are afraid, or anxious, or doubtful, or despairing, or beset by any one of those negative emotions that we experience when our life, or some bit of it, becomes difficult. But contrary to appearances, the difficulty (together with the servant's reaction to it) is only a small part of the reality here. The servant may find it hard to believe Elisha's words, "We have more on our side than they have on theirs," but he has no trouble at all when his eyes are opened. Then he sees what's really there, and what's really there is indescribably more real than what only a moment before appeared to be all there was and which had filled his eyes, his thoughts and his emotions, leaving room for nothing else. Now his eyes have been opened, and by the same God – the God for whom nothing is impossible – who soon afterwards closes the eyes of the Syrian soldiers tight shut.

Try to get a sense of movement in Luke's story of Jairus' daughter. As soon as Jesus crosses the lake, having healed a man possessed by demons, Jairus falls at his feet and begs him to come and cure his dying daughter. So Jesus sets off. There is expectancy and hope; Jesus is going to do something, and he's going to do something mightily good. However, along the way he is ambushed by a sick woman. She is healed, at once, but then they start to talk. All movement stops now, and the spotlight shifts from a dying girl somewhere off stage to a woman now centre stage, a woman whom nobody had known was there, a woman who eats up all of the precious time the little girl has left. And then the message comes: the girl is dead.

It isn't true for Jesus, but for every other person present the girl's death is a concrete reality. "Don't bother the Teacher any longer," says the messenger, implying that nobody, not even Jesus, can do anything about it now. Delivering the possessed? Apparently. Healing the sick? It seems so. Raising the dead to life? It hasn't even crossed their minds. Let the Teacher go on his way; he has more important things to do.

No, actually he hasn't. Right now, Jairus' daughter is the most important thing on Jesus' agenda, and immediately Jesus says to Jairus, in an echo of Elisha's words to his servant, "Don't be afraid; only believe, and she will be well." How can he say this? It's because as he himself is the way, the truth and the life, he knows what and where reality is, and it isn't here among a dead girl and a grieving family. It's above and beyond them, and Jesus lifts his eyes and looks up, as he always does, to a Father in whom all things are possible.

"Don't be afraid," says Jesus, even though Jairus has every reason to be afraid. He's afraid of looking at the face of his dead child, of looking into the eyes of his wife, and of living the rest of his life with a gaping hole in the middle. He may also be afraid that he's just put too much trust in a man who isn't quite what Jairus thought he was. And the trouble with fear is that it gives power to the thing we're afraid of. A spider may be small and harmless, but it's a terrifying thing to the person who's scared of it. We give it a power – and a reality – that it doesn't have, and as we do that we let it suck all the power out of us.

Jesus knows this and encourages Jairus to let go of his fear and take up belief. But a belief in what? Does the distraught father of a dead child really believe that she will live? Is it possible to summon up that kind of faith? Or is it a belief in something else, *someone* else in fact? It's not like believing that China exists, but a little like looking into the eyes of a young person (your child, maybe, or a hesitant pupil) and saying, "I believe in you." Isn't Jesus inviting Jairus not to empower what he fears by fearing it, but instead to participate in the girl's healing by trusting him, by believing he is who he says he is, by giving himself over to him? Jesus is asking for involvement, for trust, for a surge of faith that says yes to Jesus and to his reality when everything else around him screams, "No!" And perhaps surprising to almost all present, this is what Jesus gets.

Not everyone goes along with him. When Jesus arrives at the house and tells the mourners that the girl is only sleeping, they all laugh at him. Can you imagine that, laughing at Jesus? But they do. And being laughed at is a terrible thing. Other people's laughter says that we are foolish or stupid, that we are in cloud cuckoo land or away with the fairies, that we have lost our grip on reality. The ones doing the laughing are on solid ground; they are laughing at us while we sink into quicksand. Their laughter fills us with doubt, makes us question all that we were beginning to hope might be true, and causes us to avert our eyes and look down, or look inside ourselves, which is just as bad.

Jesus doesn't fall for that. He knows who he is, and he knows who his Father is. Neither does he fall into the trap of thinking that the way things appear to be is the way things have to be. Taking the girl by the hand, he calls out, "Get up, my child!" With that she opens her eyes and looks up, and it's then that we realise that the spotlight hasn't been on the little girl, and neither was it on the sick woman along the way. The spotlight has been on Jesus all the time. It's just that, as usual, we weren't looking in the right place.

DO I DARE?

Do I dare
(do you?)
even to think
that what Jesus said
just might be true?

Do I dare
to part the crowd
(there are so many!)
and say with any
confidence what I'm allowed?

Do I dare
give up the person I've become
– a character begun
in the infirmity of time,
uniquely mine?

Do I dare
to do without attention,
pass up each mention
of my strength and bravery,
considering how hard my life must be?

Do I dare
to go beyond the probability
that nothing changes?
(Better by far preserve the dream
than risk futility.)

Do I dare
to show humility,
admit, or try to, what it is I want,
look him in the eye,
say, "Over to you"?
Do I dare?
Do you?

A Prayer

Jesus,
You are the True Vine,
And I abide in you.
You are the Narrow Gate,
And I walk through with you.
You are the Good Shepherd;
I am kept safe by you.
You are the Light of the World;
My path is lit by you.
You are the Bread of Life,
And I am fed by you.
You are the Way,
And I am led by you.
You are the Truth;
I set my course by you.
You are the Resurrection and the Life;
I place my trust and hope in you.

39

Downsizing

John 1:1-14

I RECEIVED A CALL FROM A FRIEND, A RETIRED METHODIST minister who is trying to learn Spanish. One of his aids towards acquiring his new language is to do his daily reading, or part of it, from a Spanish Bible. He had called me for help. His dictionary wasn't up to the job, and could I explain the Spanish used in his translation of John 1:14, "...and Jesus dwelt among us"? For one of the Spanish words he could only find 'purple', which didn't work no matter how hard he stretched it. I was happy to explain (after checking the item myself, which I did confess to) that although this word could sometimes mean purple, in this context it meant 'dwelling place', so that my friend's version of the more usual "Jesus dwelt among us" was "Jesus put his dwelling place in the middle of us", which at first sounded rather odd.

And then I started to think that 'dwelt among us' – a phrase familiar to us from at least one reading every Christmas – may have become too familiar, and that it may be a little on the bland side. Jesus dwelling among us doesn't on the face of it say a great deal. People dwell among us for all sorts of reasons. They may move to be close to their job or to their family, but it's equally possible that they may get off the bus when their money runs out and stick around for a while because the beer's cheap. By itself, 'dwelt among us' doesn't say anything except that he dwelt among us.

My friend's Spanish version, on the other hand, says a good deal more: "He put his dwelling place in the middle of us." This isn't an accidental turning up, a just happening to be there, a sort of good idea at the time that you get over and move on from. Not at all. 'He put' means that he moved something from one place to another. It was a deliberate choice, an act of the will, a decision to do something. And what Jesus did was to move house from a place which suited him utterly to somewhere that didn't suit him at all, and he did this entirely for the sake of the people who were living there, a large number of whom, as it turned out, wished he hadn't bothered.

'Among us' isn't as good as 'in the middle of us' either. It's still vague. 'In the middle of us' leaves no room for confusion. There are no boundaries; he's right there in the middle. There are no favourites; he's rubbing shoulders with everybody. There is no escape for him; he's there in the thick of it. And being in the thick of it means that he finds himself in situations we would prefer not to be in, with people we would prefer not to be with. Prostitutes, tax collectors, women caught in adultery, lepers, sick people, foreigners, the unclean, the possessed and the dispossessed, Jesus moved his dwelling place to be in the middle of *them*, people who, on the whole, had absolutely no idea where he had moved his dwelling place from. Or why.

Now, you might think that what Jesus was doing here was, to use that now overworked phrase, moving out of his comfort zone. After all, when your home is made in the golden palaces of heaven, you're going to find it all but impossible to live in the sewer. But that's not what we find. Jesus doesn't appear to be moving out of his comfort zone at all, in that he never seems to be uncomfortable, ill at ease, with anybody. The religious leaders of the time certainly thought that he should have been, and they criticised him forcibly for associating with the wrong sort of people. But for Jesus there was no wrong sort of people, except, of course, those who thought they were the right sort of people. And he wasn't uncomfortable with them either, he just hated what they were doing to themselves and knew that the hole they were digging was such a very deep pit to be pulled out of.

I think Jesus was comfortable with people, no matter who they were, because of what he *knew*, and I mean 'knew' in that deep, unshakeable, rooted-in-our-bones sort of knew. When it came to meeting people, Jesus wasn't a labeller like we are. It wasn't a case of this leper and that tax collector. Jesus knew people as individual and unique children of God who were on the point of joyful salvation. Our habit is to judge people and to be afraid of them. Jesus didn't judge and he wasn't afraid.

And that was because he was utterly secure in himself; he knew who he was. We, on the other hand, are complicated little bundles of uncertainty as we flit, often hopelessly, from one thought and one emotion to another. Doubts, anxieties and fears fly around inside us and leave us divided against ourselves. No wonder I find it so hard to relate to others: I find it so hard to relate to myself. Jesus didn't find it hard. He knew he was the son of God and that his Father was well pleased with him. In that knowledge lay his security. Jesus says that I

225

too am a child of the Father, loved with an everlasting love, and in that, if I had any sense, I would find my security too.

Jesus knew people, and he loved them. He knew who he was too and was unshakeable in that knowledge. He knew as well, and this perhaps most importantly, who his Father was, and he knew that he could trust him everywhere and with everything. And so he had no need for comfort zones. One dwelling place was the same as another, one person the same as the next, not because people and places didn't change, but because his Father didn't change. And Jesus invites us to know as he knows, and to live in that knowledge. He invites us to live every moment knowing who we are and knowing who it is that we belong to.

The Duke of Burgundy is a small, uncommon spring butterfly. Widespread in Europe, in the UK it is found principally but not exclusively in southern counties. The subject of this poem was seen in 2018 and was one of the last, possibly the last, to be observed in that particular colony and in the county. I was very pleased, therefore, to be able to record its short life in this way.

DUKE OF BURGUNDY

May sees the coming of the Duke,
Though his arrival is, one might say, unceremonious.
He brings no retinue; no-one stands and waits
To bow and scrape, attend to every need or whim.
There is no fanfare, no pomp or circumstance,
No slaves or soldiers, not one fine feather to be seen
In all his dukedom, which, to be fair,
Extends to little more than these few yards square.
He has no country pile, no palace in the deer park,
Nothing but the tiniest fraction of what, I suppose,
Might sometimes be a park, but which, here, is a low
Hollow on the side of an unremarkable hill,
Ash- and poplar-sheltered and, occasionally, warm.
For monuments, he has a stand of nettles, for gold
The simple honesty of primroses and cowslips, for jewels
These dew-diamonds still sparkling in the morning grass,
Set randomly in crowns of scrubby thorn.
Here, then, the Duke holds court, which, today, is only me.
I kneel. I have to; he sits no more than inches
From the ground, attentive to my movements, to my gaze,
Attentive, too, to interlopers passing: flies, moths,
Anything that represents a challenge to his reign.
At each, he darts up, skirmishes a little, sees it off,
Then settles, slightly elsewhere, with a twitch of wings
And gives me his attention once again. "Now, where were we?"
We were, I think, just being, happy in each other's presence,
Me, marvelling at his acceptance of this hulking thing
Slumped like a grazing beast in his estate,
Wondering at this priceless work of art not two feet distant,
This tiny, short-lived creature painted with what seems
Extravagant and quite unnecessary beauty, and a gift,
Today at least, that is given to none but me.

But time passes, and I shuffle off
To another form of life, back down the hill to the town,
Back to cars and coffee cups and shoppers and shops,
Though it is true to say that I have been changed a little
By the quietness to be found up there on the hill,
And I am grateful, as always, for this time spent sitting still
In the generous and gentle company of His Grace.

A PRAYER

Today, and every day,

May I value my time, and avoid both idleness and over-busyness.

May I make time to be alone, both with myself and with my heavenly Father.

May I be courageous, ready at every moment to stand up for what is right and for those who are wronged.

May I show kindness and compassion, laughing with those who laugh and weeping with those who weep.

May I look to encourage, choosing to see God's vision of the best in those around me.

May I be unafraid, and open to each possible adventure.

May I live in faith and hope, walking always towards light and not darkness.

May I be secure in who I am, not dependent on the validation and opinions of others.

May I know myself to be a child of God, loved and forgiven, and may I live with confidence in my identity in him.

40

A Vision of Angels

Revelation 21:1-11,22-27

IT WAS AT THE TIME OF MY FATHER'S LAST ILLNESS, OR perhaps he had just passed away; I don't remember exactly. Neither can I tell you whether this was a vision from beyond me or the product of an over-inventive imagination. Certainly I don't recall making it up, at least not in the sense of adding one detail to another, because I remember it in my head as if the picture had arrived complete and lacking nothing. And I remember it for its otherness, an otherness beyond what one might ordinarily invent, if only for its beautiful simplicity and unexpectedness.

In this picture my father (I'm guessing it was my father, though he lay with his head nearest to me and with his face hidden, so that in effect it could have been anybody) had died and was being attended to by half a dozen people. He was wearing a white gown, and initially I had the impression that they were preparing him for burial, though I sensed after a time that they weren't getting him ready for death but for life.

The first impression I had was one of gloom, and it matched my own mood exactly. But in fact the tone of this picture was anything but gloomy, for my father's attendants were chatting and laughing together, and it was clear that what they were doing was leading towards something powerfully good. Though their age was indeterminate, they gave the impression of being teenagers, and whilst they appeared male and female one sensed that their gender was not something that mattered. They were wearing loose-fitting garments, a little like robes in the Eastern or Roman style. These clothes were of a creamy peach colour and were of such a nature that one's eyes had difficulty fixing on them. It was as if these young people were dressed in clothes made only of light.

I'm struggling for words here, but I had the impression that there was nothing here of this earth: no stain, no sharp edge and no self. Everything these attendants did, they did from pure joy and from an exuberant and totally selfless devotion. But it isn't simply that they were immersed in something beyond themselves; they themselves were beyond. Their joy, bubbling laughter and self-giving were not something that had come to them because of what they were doing (though in part it had) but because of who they were. They were a kind of people you had never met before, though perhaps you had had momentary glimpses of them in people that you knew.

I said in part, because it is also true that they were joyful on account of the person lying there, for their joy also came from an anticipation that something wonderful was going to happen. It wasn't a grave they were getting him ready for but something like a wedding celebration, and they were preparing him with such love and care and attention to detail that you couldn't be unaware of how very special this person was. There was a beautiful, childlike innocence in it all and a radiant light, not a light reflected off things but a light which shone out of things.

How can one explain this, and how can one possibly explain that these wonderful angelic beings were servants to this mortal and that they took their pleasure from this? That isn't the point, I suppose, because in reality they were taking their pleasure from serving another greater one who remained unseen but whose presence, I felt, permeated everything. And that other thing: an impression that the kind of life being lived in this scene was so far beyond our present experience that one drop of it would be worth more than the earth itself, and that it was, to the nth degree, more real than our own reality can ever be. Or, conversely, that in comparison to the otherness of that life, our own reality is little more than a shadow.

My father's last few weeks were very difficult for him, and they were hard for us too, but it would have been a very insensitive person who did not appreciate the many signs of God's mercy during my father's final stay in hospital: the generous, selfless care of hospital staff, the nurse who prayed with him in the long hours of the night, our friend the hospital chaplain who turned up, as if by chance, a few minutes before my father died and who was able to send him on his way with God's blessing. And then there was the day of the funeral, warm, sunny, open-ended, long enough to do all that we had wanted to do in the way we had wanted to do it.

Old age, as I'm beginning to discover, is a time when things begin to stop working. We were with my father when he died. We were there at precisely that point when everything stopped working, when the old life passed away, when a rather loud voice inside you tempts you to think, "Well, that's it, all gone, never to return." But that's not the voice that speaks in Revelation. The Revelation voice also tells us that the old things have gone, but it makes it very clear what these old things are: death, grief, crying and pain. As for the self, God simply makes it new. It is, after all, a New Jerusalem that is revealed to John, not the old one, and not a different city altogether but the old one made new, "like a bride dressed to meet her husband". I think it's good to know that however horrible death is, it's followed straight away by wedding bells. And who doesn't look forward to a wedding?

Thoughts on the Day After My Father's Funeral

Don't be surprised if that writing in the skies
which you have so earnestly desired
does not for one moment in your life materialise.
Don't be surprised if the encircling sun
does not step down, and like some puppet
dance before your eyes. And do not be surprised
if the uncertain road that shimmers in the haze
does not, without hint of turning, rise
laughing to meet you. Train your eyes
instead to light on smaller things:
the painful joy that sharing sadness brings,
encounters perfect though unplanned,
the welcome smile of strangers in your land.
Look instead at a woman's hand
touching the face of an old man
who falls asleep for the last time.
And notice, if you must have a sign,
that even for you the sun stood still,
and in a single day there happened,
in a slow, serene, unfolding dance,
much more than you had ever dared imagine.

A Prayer

Lord,
You are the source and end
Of all my longing,
My well of hope, my light,
My spring of life and healing.
You are my dazzling city walls,
My new beginning, my guarantee
That death and grief and pain have passed,
That tears will be for ever
Kept for love and joy and awe,
For standing, arm in arm,
With people from all nations
Before the throne of God himself,
And looking on your face
At last.

Similar Books from the Publisher

Come Away With Me
Ruth Gregg
ISBN 978-1-78815-612-7

This 90-day devotional is an excellent resource to help us effectively engage with the Bible every day. Ruth Gregg, Director of Impact Unlimited Bible College, draws our attention each day to a scripture, then clearly explains its meaning by relating it to our experiences in today's culture. Sometimes fun, always insightful, these short daily notes lead to a powerful application each day, helping us to grow into greater maturity in our relationship with the Lord.

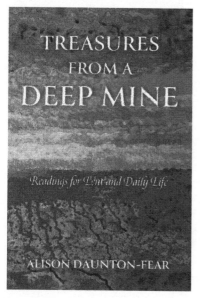

Treasures from a Deep Mine
Alison Daunton-Fear
ISBN 978-1-78815-517-5

A collection of 40 talks by Alison Daunton-Fear, a gifted preacher whose ministry spanned a large part of the twentieth century, including during the years of the Second World War. Alison's talks reflect her radiant Christian faith and beauty of spirit, her extensive knowledge of the Bible, and her deep love and understanding of the needs of humanity. They are concise but packed with spiritual truth with practical application.

www.onwardsandupwards.org/shop